Engaging
Leadership Cultures

Engaging
Leadership Cultures

David Elverson

Engaging Leadership Cultures
David Elverson

Published in the United Kingdom by Wild Horses Publishing

ISBN 978-0-9932363-0-3

Dedication

To Holly

without you letting me chase my dreams I would never
have found them

Contents

About the Author

David Elverson began life in marketing and has always been fascinated by the emotional engagement between a brand and its customers. He set up a marketing consultancy in 2004 and this merged with a more general management consultancy in 2007 with David becoming the Commercial Director. He is now a Director at Change Consultancy and the Managing Director of DEEP.

DEEP (Develop Engagement Enhance Productivity) is born from the research that David shares in this book. It is both a tool and consultancy support that develops engagement levels in an organisation and in so doing, identifies the impact on productivity and the return on investment.

For more information visit **www.engage-deep.co.uk**

CHAPTER 1

Introduction

I recently went to visit an organisation where excellence was normal. By that I don't mean they had clear processes that all staff followed to ensure high quality was attained. It was much more than that. The staff from this organisation were the most motivated and engaged group I have come across. They were so passionate about the goals, mission and values of the organisation that they gave absolutely everything to it. In return the organisation gave the staff high levels of autonomy to get on and do the job, and boy they did. The staff completely bought into the vision of the organisation, but the organisation also bought into their vision and helped each staff member to reach their potential. Their focus is on making big people because they know that if they do, they will also get big results. By focusing on making big people they have created a culture of engagement. A culture where staff have to be told to stop and rest because they are so passionate about furthering the mission of the organisation and motivated to become the best that they can be in the process. They are an example of engagement in action.

When we really 'engage' this is what happens. Staff go the extra mile because they want to, because they get something back that is actually far more motivational than a larger pay packet. When this happens our organisations also achieve greater things. It is possible to measure these engagement levels and predict the impact they will have on productivity and therefore the return on investment of doing something about it. This book will explain why and how - why engagement adds up.

Defining what I mean by engagement is important, but is actually quite difficult as there isn't a single definition for it, even though it's one of those terms that is particularly popular at the moment and used in many different contexts. Those in the workplace have probably undertaken countless staff engagement surveys. You may even have thought; I'm very / not very (delete as appropriate) engaged with (insert blank) at the moment!

My particular take is that engagement is the search for fulfilment. When individuals within a group are fulfilled, then the group or organisation will also achieve much greater things.

This book explores what engagement really is, how to engage with people better and the results that you can expect to see as a result. In essence this book is about creating an engaging culture. It is a leadership book that starts with you as an individual leader; helping you to reflect on your leadership style and the impact it has on the engagement and productivity of those you lead. From there it moves on to look at how to create engaging leadership cultures in your teams and organisations because in doing so, your results will soar.

I want to start by telling you the story of how I got into all of this. The story is important, as is yours, because our stories tell a lot about assumptions and cultures that impact on our thinking, attitude and behaviours and our ability to engage. My story begins with a problem, a passion and an interest.

The Problem

Those of us working with people know that working with them more effectively makes a difference. It must do mustn't it? Otherwise why are we doing the work we are doing and why is there such an industry of experts, consultants and gurus all plying their trade and advertising their workshops, planning tools, books and DVDs.

We know it does; just look at great teachers who find the key to getting the best out of the badly behaved child and turn them into a motivated student who goes on to achieve their potential. What about the captain of the sports team who galvanises a group of misfits into an all-conquering team that achieves far more than the sum of the parts? I'm sure you can all think of contrasts between those leaders in your workplaces who have 'got you' and you will run through brick walls for and well...let's just say the opposite kind of leader who has the opposite effect on you!

Working effectively with people works! Leading and managing people well effects how they perform and therefore the results that are generated through them. We all know this, it is certainly no great revelation and I'm sure as you have read this there has been no light bulb moment as you've thought, "Wow I never knew that"!

However, what seems obvious and 'common sense' very often appears to be not so 'common' in the workplace. The paradigm with which we view our organisations, structures and indeed management thinking actually doesn't take account of people and the way they think, work and are motivated; more of that later though. What is taken account of and, over the last decade has become increasingly important as financial pressure have led to tighter budgets, are the numbers, the bottom line.

There is nothing wrong with focusing on the bottom line, in fact if a business or any organisation operated without doing so they are probably heading for bankruptcy pretty quickly. However, the focus on the bottom line has led to a pre-eminence and focus on 'things' that have an obvious impact on the bottom line. It is relatively easy to see the impact a new IT system will have on the bottom line. A new structure can be costed and the impact on the bottom line worked through. Processes can be examined, waste identified and, with an increasing degree of accuracy, new more efficient processes can be launched with a clear impact on the bottom line.

None of this is wrong and in fact it is good...apart from one thing. By focusing on what is easy to measure we are ignoring what really makes the biggest difference on the bottom line for most organisations; the people.

This is the problem. We know that working more effectively with people delivers results, but proving that is much more difficult. In fact, because it is difficult, our organisational paradigm has moved away from it completely to focus on the more easily measurable and, in doing so, has actually created a culture that effects people adversely and gets less from them.

The problem we need to solve is how to demonstrate the impact that engagement and engaging leadership has on the bottom line in a language that the accountants and the CFOs will understand and take notice of.

The Passion

Over the last thirteen years as a consultant I've worked in at least two different organisations every week. If you add in the workshops that I also run, again probably averaging one or two a week, then I have had contact with a large workforce. This has been great as I get bored easily and the variety that I've found in working in different organisations has been incredibly stimulating. There have been huge differences between these businesses and yet there are several themes that seem common to all organisations I've worked with and cut across all sectors. One of these themes is that there are so many people in the workforce who are not fulfilled. They have become human robots held captive by the culture and ultimately their own expectations.

This saddens me as a person and frustrates the life out of me as a consultant who is charged with helping organisations increase their productivity. This culture isn't good for the individuals and it certainly isn't good for the business. People who aren't fulfilled don't work hard. They may seem to and they may put in the hours needed, but their heart and soul isn't in the work. In one sense you could say, "Why should it be? They are paid to do a job and as long as they get it done then they don't need to give any more".

There is truth in that, but actually we can all have so much more. Releasing people to thrive not only makes work a better place for the individuals, but it also leads to increased performance for the organisation.

Giving their all doesn't mean working longer or harder. However if they are engaged and feel they are being fulfilled and have purpose in what they are doing, then they will certainly work more effectively.

My passion is to see this become the normal way of working. Work doesn't have to be about survival to pay the bills until you can really live at the weekend or when you retire. Work can be invigorating and fulfilling and when it is, the organisation reaps the benefits as well as the individual.

When this becomes the culture the impact on the bottom line is so obvious and noticeable that the problem will change. It will now be "why didn't we do this before"!

The Interest

I've always been interested in people and the way they function. I started my career in marketing and was particularly fascinated with the emotional engagement that occurs between brands and their customers.

A great example of this are Apple geeks (I apologize if you are one of the people I am about to describe). They queue through the night to be one of the first people to get hold of the latest iphone or ipad. That isn't logical or rational! They could wander into the store a few days later and pick it up without going through the discomfort of queuing through the night on a cold pavement, possibly with rain pouring down on them. They do it because of an incredibly strong emotional engagement to the brand. This emotional engagement is far more powerful than the rational part of them that is saying "don't be stupid, I can get a good night's sleep, stay warm and dry and get my new phone next week"!

This is at the heart of a strong brand, the emotional connection between the brand and the customer. Advertisers have known this for years. Next time you are looking at the adverts watch out for the ones advertising cars. A decade ago or so they were all about the features and the benefits of the cars. Now they are all about the life you will have if you own a car like that. People will look at you a certain way if you own that particular car! They are playing on our emotions because they know that we make decisions because of these strong emotions.

Over the last few years I've been actively looking to apply the same sophistication of thinking to our workforces, not just our customers. After all, people are people and the way we are motivated into action is the same whatever that action is; whether it is to buy something or to work hard.

This search for information led me to the field of behavioural economics and inquiry into the boundaries between psychology and economics. At the same time as undertaking this search I was in a period of consultancy that seemed to involve a large number of economic impact assessments, cost benefit analysis and return on investment analysis projects. The themes seemed to merge. The problem of demonstrating the impact working with people has and my passion to see people fulfilled in the workplace, and in so doing, achieving greater levels of performance, found a home in understanding the economics of our behaviour.

Behavioural Economics

Our economy, our organisational structures and much of our management thinking is based on the neo-classical economic view. This is a presumption that we are rational people who make rational decisions. This isn't true. We are all on a spectrum with some of us more rational and some of us more emotional, but for the average person, 70% 0f the decisions they make comes from an emotional place not a rational one. This could be something like: wanting to be included, being recognised or being part of something. None of these are wrong, but they aren't necessarily rational either.

A few years ago, neuroscientist Antonio Damasio made a ground breaking discovery. He studied people with damage in the part of the brain where emotions are generated. He found that, aside from not being able to feel emotions, they seemed normal. But they all had something peculiar in common: they couldn't make decisions. They could describe what they should be doing in logical terms, yet they found it very difficult to make even simple decisions, such as what to eat.

This discovery showed that our emotions are vital to making decisions, even everyday ones. The more complex a decision, the more important our emotions become and the less important the logic and rationale.

Let's put this to the test. I want you to imagine the following scenario:

You are on your way to the airport to go on a holiday of a lifetime. You are off to the Maldives and you have seen the brochure of where you are going. You will have your own private beach front apartment on a white sandy beach with the waves lapping just in front of your sun kissed terrace. It will be beautifully hot and you can laze about all day if you want, or if you prefer, then there are water sports and adventures to be had. Whatever your dream holiday is you are about to go on it.

You are on the way to the airport and your car breaks down. You call the breakdown services and at this point, there are two different scenarios.

Scenario 1 - the break down service takes about two hours to get to you. They look at your car and can't fix it. You decide to go to the airport anyway just in case your flight has been delayed. They haul your car onto the back of the tow truck and take you to the airport. You push the car into a parking bay, grab your bags and rush through to departures. It isn't much of a surprise for you to find you have missed your flight by two hours.

Scenario 2 – the break down service gets to you remarkably quickly. They look at your car and manage to fix it and get you back on the road. The traffic is really heavy and it's touch and go as to whether you will make the flight or not. You arrive at the airport, park the car, grab your luggage and rush through to departures only to find that you have missed your flight by two minutes.

I want you now to think which of the scenarios would make you more frustrated and you have three options:

- Option 1 – scenario 1, missing the flight by two hours would make you more frustrated

- Option 2 – scenario 2, missing the flight by two minutes would make you more frustrated

- Option 3 – you would be equally frustrated. You missed your flight either way so there would be no difference to your levels of frustration.

Which did you go for? I've used this scenario in workshops with thousands of people and in total, about 70% go for option 2, about 29% go for option 3 and a very small number go for option 1.

The rational answer is option 3. You missed the flight so you've missed it. However for the majority of people it's easier to imagine what it would have been like when you only just miss it, than when you miss it by a long way. This is an emotional response. It's not a wrong response, or a right response, but it's how most of us are wired to think and make decisions.

Behavioural economics has shown us that to engage with people in a way that wins over their hearts and minds we have to understand their emotional decision making, not just the rational. The drive for productivity with the focus on process, structure and system has done the exact opposite. It is locked into the neo-classical rational view. Any change always has a great business case that makes a clear rational case. However, that might not be as important for the individual as the fact that they will no longer be sitting next to the person they enjoy sitting next to. How can you compare the two? Of course the business case is important and needed, but if we want people to roll up their sleeves and make our businesses cases and strategies work, then we need to understand what really makes them tick and engage them at that level. That is how you create a culture that fulfils people and delivers better results.

The academic studies are stacking up to prove this, although it isn't yet seeping into mainstream organisational culture in a way that has dramatic effects. Following are a few examples:

The higher employees daily engagement the higher their objective financial returns[1]

Top 25% on an engagement index out of 65 businesses from various sectors, had greater profitability, greater return on assets and over double the shareholder value compared to the bottom 25%[2]

Companies that follow behavioural economic principles outperformed their competitors by 85% in sales growth and over 25% in gross margin[3]

The financial measures of productivity used in the examples above could be exchanged for any other measure of productivity and the same would hold true. The following extract from Bakker[4] gives a great overview of the research demonstrating the impact *engagement has on results:*

There are at least four reasons why engaged workers perform better than nonengaged workers. First, engaged employees often experience positive emotions, including gratitude, joy, and enthusiasm. These positive emotions seem to broaden people's thought–action repertoire, implying that they constantly work on their personal resources[5]. Second, engaged workers experience better health. This means that they can focus and dedicate all their skills and energy resources to their work. Third, engaged employees create their own job and personal resources. Finally, engaged workers transfer their engagement to others in their immediate environment[6]. Since in most organizations performance is the result of collaborative effort, the engagement of one person may transfer to others and indirectly improve team performance.

To date, several studies have shown that work engagement is positively related to job performance (e.g., in-role performance, that is, officially required outcomes and behaviors that directly serve the goals of the organization; creativity; organizational citizenship behavior). For example, Bakker, Demerouti, and Verbeke showed that engaged employees received higher ratings from their colleagues on in-role and extra-role performance (discretionary behaviors on the part of an employee that are believed to directly promote the effective functioning of an organization, without necessarily directly influencing a person's target productivity), indicating that engaged employees perform well and are willing to go the extra mile. Further, in their study of employees working in Spanish restaurants and hotels, Salanova, Agut, and Peiró[7] showed that employee ratings of organizational resources, engagement, and service climate were positively related to customer ratings of employee performance and customer loyalty.

In their recent study of Greek employees working in fastfood restaurants, Xanthopoulou, Bakker, Demerouti, and Schaufeli[8] expanded this research and made a compelling case for the predictive value of work engagement for performance on a daily basis. Participants were asked to fill in a survey and a diary booklet for 5 consecutive days. Consistent with hypotheses, results showed that employees were more engaged on days that were characterized by many job resources. Daily job resources like supervisor coaching and team atmosphere contributed to employees' personal resources (day levels of optimism, self-efficacy, and self-esteem), which, in turn, contributed to daily engagement. Importantly, this study clearly showed that engaged employees perform better on a daily basis. The higher employees' levels of daily engagement, the higher their objective financial returns.

Good engagement understands emotional decision making points and 'engages' with people at these points. That's what the best brands do. That's what Apple have managed to do with many of their customers to turn them into an army of advocates that are willing to put themselves through relative discomfort just to get a new product before everyone else. The best organisations also do this with their staff. They engage with their staff at such a deep emotional level that the staff love working there, they feel empowered, happy, and motivated and go the extra mile for the organisation.

Thinking into action

From the problem, the passion and the interest I decided to take some positive action to try and create something that would raise 'people' further up the agenda and in so doing, help organisations become more productive.

I undertook a large literature review of any academic work I could find in the fields of: motivation, behaviour change, engagement, behavioural economics and many other areas. From this I developed two models. The first is a distilled version of what really matters or what really makes someone engaged. The academics used different terms and had some slight differences. I brought these together to identify eight areas of engagement that seem to be important and there is broad agreement over. I also noticed a growing body of evidence that showed a clear link between engagement and productivity. There were quite a few variables at play, but drawing on my rusty A Level maths to begin with and then later on the assistance of two Cambridge mathematician friends, I created an algorithm that measures how engaged people are, the impact this engagement has on productivity and therefore the return on investment an organisation will see if they engage their staff more.

Now this may be boring to some of you who aren't involved in the corporate world, but it was actually described as 'the golden bullet' by one HR Director. The model that I created now enabled an organisation to clearly see the impact their 'people initiatives' were having and therefore gave insight to invest in the right areas to see a return on that investment.

I turned this research into an online tool called DEEP with associated consultancy support and spun it off under a different brand name, separate from Change Consultancy to keep the brand messages clear.

The Culture of Engagement

Following is a short summary of the eight areas. There is a chapter on each of these areas that looks at them in much greater depth and offers practical thoughts and ideas on how to develop these cultures in your personal leadership style and in your teams and organisations.

Meaning

We are engaged when we see an alignment between our personal values and those in our workplace. Leon Festinger in his Cognitive Dissonance Theory[9] proposes that people feel uncomfortable when they feel a clash or dissonance between their actions and attitudes or values. This thinking has been taken further by Lips-Wiersma and Morris[10] in their work The Map of Meaning. They suggest engagement is only possible when an individual can see alignment between their personal values and the formal and informal values of a workplace.

Habits

Our habits are stronger than our intentions. This influences our behaviour whether we want it to or not. Cialdini[11] writes how routinised behaviour becomes detached from the original motivating factors; changing those factors (eg. attitudes or intentions) will not necessarily change the habit, as their power in influencing the behaviour has become attenuated. In this dynamic, habitual behaviours can be seen to bypass deliberative processes. Trandis[12] describes how, as experience of a behaviour is acquired, the influence of habit increases, and that of intention declines. A similar dynamic is at play in the Prototype/Willingness Model from health psychologists Gibbons and Gerrard.[13]

In the workplace; team and organisational habits in the way we think and solve problems can reduce personal engagement and individual habits can stop engagement and productivity despite the best intentions.

Influences

We are influenced by other people. This isn't a rational conscious decision, it just occurs. In the workplace this happens at two main levels: we are influenced by the culture that exists and by the people we spend the most time with. Put simply, *"Norms guide how we should behave"*[14] .

Self-Expectations

The way we think about ourselves and what we are able to achieve has a large impact on our engagement. Higgin's self-discrepancy theory[15] says we have three views of ourselves: actual, ideal and ought-self (what we ought to be like). We also have perceptions of how others see us against these three levels. Differences between these different views can give rise to negative emotions such as guilt and disappointment that impact on our engagement.

We are also limited by our own expectations, if we don't think we can achieve something, we probably won't (Bandura self-efficacy theory[16]).

Loss

Kahneman and Tversky[17] showed that people are not impartial to whether a loss or a gain is involved; they put more effort into preventing loss that winning a gain. This has particular consequence when organisations are changing. Typically we are good at 'selling the benefits' of the change, but this often isn't as important to people as reflecting on what they have lost.

The implication for engagement is that understanding perceived loss helps you to understand the impact loss has on engagement.

Leadership Characteristics

Engagement is about emotional decision making and emotional decision making is highly influenced by our relationships as we are social beings. I have already mentioned that our relationships with peers affect us (influences). It therefore stands to reason that our relationships with leaders also impact on our engagement.

Gallup[18] has undertaken interesting work on the characteristics of leaders that result in the most engaged staff. The characteristics they found to be most important were; Trust, Hope Compassion and Stability.

Trust

The chances of an employee being engaged at work when they do not trust the company's leaders are 1 in 12, the chances of an employee being engaged in work when they do trust the leaders are 1 in 2

Compassion

Staff who agree with the statement: "My manager seems to care about me as a person" are: Significantly more likely to stay with the organisation, have more engaged customers, are substantially more productive and produce better outcomes for the organisation.

Stability

Followers want leaders who will provide a solid foundation even through times of change. Employees who have high confidence in their organisation's financial future are nine times as likely to be engaged in their jobs than those with a lower confidence.

Hope

Employees want hope for the future. 69% of employees who 'feel enthusiastic about the future' are engaged in their jobs compared to 1% who are not enthusiastic.

Strengths

We are motivated by doing things we are good at. It sounds obvious but the majority of organisations focus on weaknesses and developing them. Rath and Conchie and before them Donald Clifton and Marcus Buckingham in their book, 'Now discover your strengths' highlight research demonstrating the impact focusing on strengths has on engagement and productivity.

Involvement

Bandura's theory on self-efficacy argues that our perceived capability to achieve a level of performance affects our behaviour. This affects the choices we make, our effort levels and how long we stick at something before giving up. Kaplan takes this further by suggesting that telling people what to do reduces their self-efficacy and leaving people unsure as to why their effort is needed to achieve the bigger picture also reduces their self-efficacy.

Therefore the involvement people have in decisions that impact on them and their understanding of why they and their actions are important to the bigger picture, impacts on their engagement.

Engaging Leadership

Through the tool I developed, DEEP, I have inadvertently created a rich research base through which we can further examine what engages people and the impact it has. The most conclusive, of the many findings we have made, is that the single biggest factor that affects the engagement levels in an organisation, is the leadership culture that exists. If this is what impacts on engagement levels then it is also what impacts on productivity levels.

An engaging leadership culture takes account of the emotional decisions that people make. The eight areas of engagement are intertwined into an engaging way of leading across the organisation. When this happens, productivity increases. The remaining chapters of the book will explore the eight areas of engagement in more depth giving practical thoughts and insights into how to develop your own leadership style and how to create an increasingly engaging culture across your organisation.

The book is designed to be used by you as an individual, looking to increase the engagement and performance of your team. It is even more effective if used across a management team and together you look to create an engaging culture that sees individuals fulfilled and the bottom line going up

References

1 Xanthopoulou, D., Bakker, A.B., Demerouti, E., & Schaufeli, W.B. (2009a). *Reciprocal relationships between job resources, personal resources, and work engagement. Journal of Vocational Behavior, 74, 235–44.*

2 Macey, W.H., Schneider, B., Barbera, K., & Young, S.A. (2009). *Employee engagement: Tools for analysis, practice, and competitive advantage. London, England: Blackwell.*

3 http://www.gallup.com/services/170954/behavioral-economics.aspx

4 Bakker, A.B., Albrecht, S., & Leiter, M.P. (2011). *Key questions regarding work engagement. European Journal of Work and Organizational Psychology, 20, 4–28.*

5Fredrickson, B.L. (2001). *The role of positive emotions in positive psychology: The broaden-and-build theory of positive emotions. American Psychologist, 56, 218–226.*

6 Bakker, A.B., & Xanthopoulou, D. (2009). *The crossover of daily work engagement: Test of an actor–partner interdependence model. Journal of Applied Psychology, 94, 1562–1571.*

7 Salanova, M., Agut, S., & Peiró, J.M. (2005). *Linking organizational resources and work engagement to employee performance and customer loyalty: The mediation of service climate. Journal of Applied Psychology, 90, 1217–1227.*

8 Xanthopoulou, D., Bakker, A.B., Demerouti, E., & Schaufeli, W.B. (2009b). *Work engagement and financial returns: A diary study on the role of job and personal resources. Journal of Occupational and Organizational Psychology, 82, 183–200.*

9 Festinger, L. (1962). *"Cognitive dissonance". Scientific American 207 (4): 93–107.* doi:10.1038/scientificamerican1062-93.

10 Lips-Wiersma, M. & Morris, L. (2011) *The Map of Meaning Greenleaf, Sheffield*

11 Cialdini, R, R Reno and C Kallgren 1990. *A focus theory of normative conduct: Recycling the concept of norms to reduce littering in public places. Journal of Personality and Social Psychology 58(6) 1015-1026.*

12 Trandis, H 1977. *Interpersonal Behaviour. Monterey, CA: Brooks/Cole.*

13 Gibbons, R, M Gerrard & G Lane 2003. *A Social Reaction Model of Adolescent Health Risk. In Social Psychological Foundations of Health and Illness, eds. J Suls and K Wallston. Oxford: Blackwell.*

14 McKenzie-Mohr, D 2000. *Promoting Sustainable Behavior: An Introduction to Community-Based Social Marketing. Journal of Social Issues 56 (3), 543-554.*

15 Higgins, E.T., Roney, C.J.R., Crowe, E., Hymes C. (1994). *Ideal versus ought predilections for approach and avoidance: Distinct self-regulatory systems, Journal of Personality and Social Psychology, 66, 276-286.*

16 Bandura, A 1977. *Self-efficacy: toward a unifying theory of behavioral change. Psychological Review 84, 191–215.*

17 Kahneman, D 2002. *Maps of Bounded Rationality: a Perspective on Intuitive Judgment and Choice. Nobel Prize Lecture, December 2002.*

18 Rath, T. & Conchie, B (2008) *Strength Based Leadership, Gallup Press*

CHAPTER 2

Meaning

Having a vision and finding purpose

Deriving a sense of purpose in what we do and why we do it is so important. Finding meaning and having a vision that we are working towards motivates us and often gives us the strength to keep on going, even if things seem tough. Learning to live in a meaningful and purposeful way with a vision inspiring us and guiding us on is the first of the eight areas of engagement we are exploring.

When we see an alignment between our values and the, formal and informal, values of the organisations we are involved with, then we are engaged, motivated and brought into life.

I've recently been involved in the merger of three large businesses. They are all well-known brands and were merged to form a market leader in the UK. My specific involvement was in the post-merger culture change work to try and forge a single organisation rather than three different ones operating under the same brand.

The new company had a markedly different purpose than two of the original companies. This had a very obvious effect on the staff, both for good and bad. On the positive side, the lead company on the merger, and the one under whose brand name the new organisation traded, was a well-respected brand that stands for quality. This company expects a quality service and this is underpinned through a comprehensive set of values that articulates expectations for each job role in the organisation. The purpose of providing a high end, quality and respected service had an effect on the staff from the other two companies. They were influenced positively by being associated with the purpose of this brand.

There was also a more negative impact the merger had. The focus of the leading brand was to work with a more wealthy set of clients in order to create greater shareholder value. This was very different to the historic client group of the other two companies. Traditionally they had worked with clients who received state help. There was an interesting and marked difficulty of the staff from the other two companies to buy into the vision of the leading brand. The meaning many staff had found; of providing important services to those who couldn't afford them any other way, was being challenged. Their meaning was no longer in alignment with the purpose of the new organisation.

This alignment, or lack of alignment, is important to think about before considering what vision is, because our visions can either bring people to life or have the opposite effect.

Have you ever been in a situation where what you were hearing and seeing was so different to your experiences that it actually made you feel stressed? A slightly harder question to answer, because it happens more subtly is; have you ever noticed yourself creating justifications to explain things that are at odds with what you are seeing and experiencing? And on reflection, noticed that the justifications are more unbelievable than the original event you are trying to justify?

The banking crisis badly affected many of the clients of the consultancy I was working for at the time. We were a small, but highly respected boutique consultancy that specialised in small to medium sized change projects. Over a period of about three months these jobs seemed to dry up. Clients weren't looking for small consultancy projects, they were now looking for whole organisational change programmes and wanted the trusted name of one of the big five to deliver the work for them.

The change happened so quickly that it was at complete odds with our experience. Up until that point business had been good and growing rapidly. Over the course of a few months that had changed considerably. These events were such a contrast to our experiences of the previous three years that some of our justifications and predictions for what the market would do were actually far more unbelievable than the truth; the market had significantly changed and we had to survive.

A really interesting piece of work was undertaken by Leon Festinger[1] in the 1950s that explains these natural human reactions. His work, the theory of cognitive dissonance, showed that humans strive for internal consistency. When inconsistency (dissonance) is experienced, individuals can become psychologically distressed, or stressed as we would call it. His work led him to two key hypotheses:

- "The existence of dissonance (inconsistency with experiences and world view), being psychologically uncomfortable, will motivate the person to try to reduce the dissonance and achieve consonance"

- "When dissonance is present, in addition to trying to reduce it, the person will actively avoid situations and information which would likely increase the dissonance"

This means we find experiences that are at odds with our previous experiences and expectations stressful and try to avoid them.

He also found that the amount of dissonance, or inconsistency, and the subsequent stress is dependent on an interesting variable:

- *The importance*: The more the experience is valued, the greater the dissonance and stress.

This means that 'dissonance' or stress is particularly prevalent when the event we are experiencing is at odds with something that we value. An example of this would be someone who had very strong environmental values working at an unethical mining company whose inherent values were to exploit the environment. The values of the individual would be so different to the formal and particularly informal values of the mining company, thus creating inconsistency and leading to high levels of stress.

The work my firm and others have done in the field of engagement has demonstrated the impact of alignment of values. The meaning and purpose a person has, and in particular its alignment to the formal and informal values, purpose and vision of the organisation the person is a part of, has a large impact on how engaged someone is and therefore the fullness of life they experience whilst at work. Dan Pink, in his excellent book Drive[2], came to the same conclusion. He identified three factors that influence our intrinsic motivation; autonomy, mastery and purpose. His definition of purpose is very similar to this. He found that we need to have a purpose and we need to see an alignment between that purpose and what we are actually doing at work in order to be motivated.

This is why vision is so important: people having a vision and purpose is motivational and brings people alive. We need a vision and we need to lead others in a way so they develop their own vision. When we are leading people we need to realise the impact our vision and underlying values have on those around us. If they are different from their experiences, expectations and values it actually creates dissonance for them, or as we would commonly experience it; stress.

Festinger's theory is also based on an assumption that people seek consistency between their expectations and reality. Because of this, people engage in a process called dissonance reduction to bring their thoughts, expectations and actions in line with one another. This creation of uniformity allows for less stress.

This reduction can happen in four different ways. Let's have a look at how this plays out in an everyday situation:

Imagine you decided to go on a diet and you are going to avoid high fat foods; however you are in a supermarket and you smell some freshly cooked doughnuts. You buy a doughnut and eat it. There is an immediate dissonance there; you plan to avoid fatty foods but you find yourself eating a doughnut. The four ways we can reduce this dissonance are as follows:

1. Change our behaviour - we stop eating the doughnut remembering how important it is that we avoid fatty foods.

2. Justify behaviour by changing the conditions - "I'm allowed to eat a doughnut once in a while."

3. Justify behaviour by adding new conditions - "I'll spend 30 extra minutes at the gym to work it off."

4. Ignore/deny any information that conflicts with existing beliefs -"I did not eat that doughnut. I always eat healthily."

Which one of these four reactions do you find yourself falling into? Knowing the way our minds work is important so that we can purposefully operate, think and act in the way we want to, not the way we end up doing. I think most of us have tendencies to one or more of these reactions and our tendency is often a learnt behaviour from our childhood.

The reason I've started this chapter on meaning with this look at cognitive dissonance is because it is so important to understand the impact our vision and values have on those we lead. It is also useful to understand why we react to situations in the way that we do.

Understanding this powerful effect of the human mind allows us to lead in a way that builds a united team, empowers others into their own vision and ultimately creates motivated people who are happy in work and performing better.

If our vision and values are at odds with the personal vision and values of those we lead it will create a dissonance in them that they will react to in different ways. However if we can lead in a way that empowers them into their own vision, helps them realise their potential and creates a confidence that they can achieve their expectations, then we are developing a culture for them to live a full and productive life that is good for them and good for the business.

What is vision?

Vision is seeing the future that you are working towards before it is a reality.   It is a bridge between the present and the future.   A metaphor for vision and change that I often use in workshops is the Oregon Trail.

The Oregon Trail migration is one of the most important events in American History. The Oregon Trail was a 2,170 mile route from Missouri to Oregon and California that enabled the migration of the early pioneers to the western United States. The first emigrants to make the trip were Marcus and Narcissa Whitman who made the journey in 1836. However, the first mass migration did not occur until 1843 when approximately 1000 pioneers made the journey at one time.

This trail was the only feasible land route for settlers to get to the West Coast. From 1843 until 1869 when the first transcontinental railroad was completed, there were over 500,000 people who made the trip in covered wagons pulled by mule and oxen. Some went all the way to Oregon to farm and others went to California to search for gold. The trip usually took 4-6 months by wagon traveling 15 miles a day. The only other route to the west, by sea, took a full year.

Stories from the early fur trappers and missionaries came back to the east coast and the mid-west of just how good the agricultural land was, how much space there was and the riches that were possible by moving to Oregon.   Later on, after gold was discovered in California in 1848, stories of great wealth also came back.

Those who set out on the Oregon Trail had a clear vision of the future; that of a better life and great wealth.   It was this vision that would keep them going through all of the hardship that they would doubtless face whilst undertaking such a mammoth journey.

In the early spring, emigrant campers would congregate around Independence, Missouri and set up camp, waiting for the grass to grow along the Oregon Trail. While waiting, the emigrants would stock up on supplies, try to locate friends, and make other preparations for their journey. If they left too early there would be no grass for their animals to eat which could be a fatal mistake. If they left too late they would get caught by the winter snows.

Most settlers travelled in farm wagons, four feet by ten feet, with a thousand pounds of food. These wagons had cotton covers treated with linseed oil to keep the rain out. Many were equipped with tool boxes, water containers, and spare axles. A broken axle on the rough trail was not an uncommon occurrence and without a spare it would mean having to abandon the wagon.

When the time finally came to leave, the settlers would all try to leave at once creating a massive traffic jam. This was further hindered by the inexperience and slow progress of some of the east coast teams. As their traveling progressed, most realised they had over packed and were forced to lighten their loads by discarding belongings and provisions along the way. Because of the heavy loads, many were forced to walk the 2,170 mile journey instead of ride in the wagon.

Imagine turning up in Independence Missouri having already left many of your possessions behind, only to find that you had to get rid of even more to make the journey because either they wouldn't fit in the wagon or it made the wagons too heavy. The vision of the future had to be strong to keep people going through the emotional and practical challenges this would have caused.

There were many accidents along the way. Getting run over by one of the wagons resulted in almost certain death for the unfortunate settler. Wounds from accidental gun shots were an all too common occurrence due to people falling around or from half-cocked pistols in the wagons. Another problem for the travellers was Cholera. Some wagon trains lost two-thirds of their people to this quick killing disease. Bodies were usually left on the side of the road or buried in shallow graves which allowed animals to dig them up and scatter their bones along the trail. This proved to be very unnerving for many of the pioneers. Again, the vision of the future had to be strong to keep people going, and even to start out in the first instance with these stories of adversity and tragedy getting back to those who were yet to commence their journeys.

A major danger to the settlers was weather. Traveling in the summer meant dealing with thunder storms, lightening and hail. Many were killed by lightning or hail the size of baseballs. All in all, one in ten did not survive the journey.

The final third of the trail was the most difficult and had to be done with expediency. Winter snows would close the mountain passes and travel was a race against time. In the early years, before the Barlow Road was opened, travellers would have to abandon their wagons for boats and float down the Columbia River. Many lost their lives in the rapids and rough parts just miles from their destination. After 1846, and upon paying a toll, the pioneers could finish their journey by crossing the Cascades on the Barlow Road.

Once in Oregon and California, settlers would start a new life and build farms or set off to the gold mines.

The vision of the future that the early travellers had was what kept them going through the hardship and what encouraged them to make the sacrifice in the first place. The strength of the vision had to be compelling enough for them to endure the hardship and risk what they knew they would likely encounter on the way. The size of the vision determines the sacrifice that people will make.

For these pioneers the vision was long term. People had a vision for their whole lives being changed, not just for a bit of a difference for the next couple of years. The long term nature of their visions had a large impact on their willingness to sacrifice in order to achieve it.

Vision must be strong before strategy is created. By that I mean we must know the 'why' and the 'what' before we start to think about the 'how'. Many times I've worked with organisations that have inhibited their vision by starting to think about how something can be achieved. This shrinks our vision and ultimately makes it less compelling. Do you think those travellers along the Oregon trail would have bothered if the vision was of a *slightly* better life?

Where does vision come from?

A lot of my work recently has been helping 'strategic planning' teams develop their 'strategic thinking'. There is a subtle yet fundamental difference between the two. Strategic thinking is looking ahead into the future to think about the 'why' and the 'what' questions whilst strategic planning focuses on 'how' we get there. Most organisations are very good at the planning but pretty bad at the thinking. This is because strategic planning is much easier and more comfortable. It is typically short term, logical, pragmatic and creates alignment between different strands of thinking. Strategic thinking, on the other hand, is much more difficult and uncomfortable. It is typically much longer term, uncertain, divergent and incomplete. However it is exactly this type of thinking that is needed to develop the type of compelling vision that people will endure personal sacrifice to follow.

To encourage strategic thinking and the creation of long term vision I encourage teams to think big, deep and long. Thinking in this way is useful whatever type of vision we are creating.

Thinking big

All too often we think too small and our visions are too small. Thinking big is seeing beyond our own organisation to the wider systems we are part of. We need to understand the impact others have on us and the impact we can also have on others. What impacts will your strategy have on others? What changes in other systems will impact on you? We need to understand the wider systems we are part of and the interdependencies that exist to move away from silo or tribal thinking.

Thinking Deep

We make assumptions all of the time and these assumptions have a large impact on the decisions that we make, our expectations for what we will achieve and what is possible. Our assumptions are usually based on our past experiences. As such these assumptions can often encase us in the past, whereby we view the world through a particular lens that is shaded by the different experiences we have had. We often don't realise our lens is shaded, or even sometimes scratched, and therefore don't realise the assumptions we are making.

When developing vision it is really important to identify the assumptions that are impacting on our thinking. The assumptions might prove to be right, but never the less, understanding they are assumptions and not necessarily reality, is very important. A good test to identify the assumptions you are making is to reflect back on times when you've had an idea or someone has put an idea to you and you've thought; 'that won't work', 'that's a crazy idea' or 'I couldn't do that'. When you've identified times like this then try and identify what the assumptions are that are underpinning your reaction.

Thinking Long

In my experience of supporting organisations with their strategic thinking, the planning is often undertaken as follows:

- we plan for a single future that is developed after we have done lots of data analysis and produced lots of trend analysis,

- we do that by extrapolating those trends into the future (that is, we use the past and present to create the future),

And

- we don't often identify and question our assumptions about the future – we maintain an official future that already exists.

This is missing an awful lot! The future might not follow the same pattern as current events and the past. In our thinking and visions we need to think beyond linear progression and we need to think much longer.

When big, deep and long creates dissonance

When our visions are big, deep and long it can automatically create a dissonance, or inconsistency with our experience and those we are leading. Their experience could be that we haven't seen turnover increase for the last five years and certainly not profit levels. Therefore a vision of increasing turnover by 25% and profit levels by 15% would be so far from the experiences of the staff that dissonance is created.

Why is vision important?

The importance of vision is put very starkly in the Proverb; '*where there is no vision, the people perish*'. In some versions of the bible the word 'vision' is translated as 'revelation'. This suggests that for us to lead our people in a way in which they thrive, our vision must include revelation on how it will be achieved.

Vision gives purpose and meaning. When we see the bigger picture the hard work of achieving it is worthwhile because there is a purpose to it. The travellers on the Oregon Trail had a purpose that certainly gave them hope. When we have hope we also have peace during the hardship of achieving the vision. It helps us to endure the sacrifice to make these visions become reality. We press on towards the prize because we know just how amazing the prize is and we have such hope and confidence that we will get it! Having vision actually gives us direction and fulfilment through difficult times of change, even when we haven't actually achieved the vision yet.

Developing vision

I use the following process when developing vision. Try it and see how it works for you:

1. Find a peaceful place and have a notebook at hand.

2. Remove any interruptions, particularly the phone, email and social media.

3. Dream about what you want to achieve personally and for your team and organisation.

4. Write down your vision in detail. Write it in the present tense, as though it has already happened. This will make it more believable to you.

5. Test what you have written down. Is it big, deep and long? What assumptions have led to it and did you discount anything you thought about before writing it down based on an assumption?

6. Share your vision with the people who have a stake in the outcome. Ask for their thoughts, insight and wisdom on it.

7. Commit to reading your vision daily.

Leading others into their vision

To lead others into a place of engagement you need to also give them permission to develop their own vision. Our traditional view of leadership is that the leader has the vision of where the organisation is going. A key role of the leader is to then communicate this vision so that everyone else buys into it and works towards it. The leader envisions the followers so together they effectively achieve the vision set out. I call that 'above the line leadership' and it can be described by the diagram below:

The Leader's vision

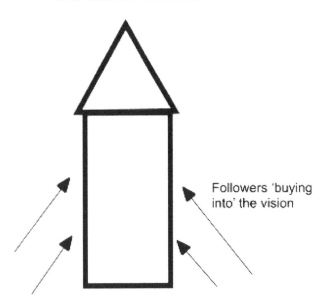

Followers 'buying into' the vision

This form of leadership is great for getting things done quickly and starting things. However, it creates followers, and thus by definition produces dependency. The level of 'buy in' to the vision is determined by factors such as: how good the vision is perceived to be, how well the leader is liked and trusted and whether the vision fits with the follower's view. If the buy in isn't good then the productivity won't be either.

What if instead of creating followers we created leaders? What if instead of envisioning others to our vision, we released them into their own vision? The result is engaged and motivated people who are empowered as leaders. They have a purpose and autonomy to become masters in their area; all key factors in motivation.

The Leader's vision

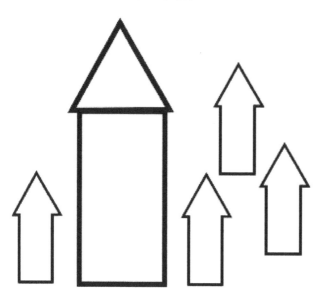

This is a very different paradigm for most businesses. Most have a leader who creates vision and staff who follow the vision and turn it into reality. There is nothing wrong with that model, but it doesn't get the best out of people and release them to be all that they can be. It in effect controls people towards a common goal. Releasing people into their own vision is risky and goes against common wisdom, but the rewards are enormous.

Google are a great example of this principle working in action. A few years ago Google gave all staff half a day to work on discretionary projects, the ideas they may have had and thought; "wouldn't it be nice if I had time to try that". This proved to be so successful that nowadays all employees at Google spend one to two days a week on these discretionary projects and the rest of their time on business as usual. It is through these discretionary projects that nearly all of Google's main products have been invented and developed. The whole company is more successful by helping staff to develop their own vision.

The staff at Google are given autonomy to get on with their ideas. They become masters in the area they are working on and derive a real purpose through the work. The result is motivated employees who are achieving great things for themselves and the company.

Sometimes the vision of people is to serve the vision of another leader. That is excellent and in fact is very common. Many people don't want to be 'the boss' but actually have a vision to serve someone else's vision that they understand and buy into. However it is very different when someone discovers that their vision is to serve, compared to someone who doesn't even realise they could have their own vision.

There is obviously a balance to be struck because we are given targets and objectives and we need to achieve them and are paid to develop a workforce that puts in the work needed to achieve these targets. We need to give staff permission to think about how they can achieve their targets, which may be a different way than we would. We also need to actively encourage them to think beyond the targets to what else is possible and what else could be achieved.

References

1. Festinger, L. (1957) A Theory of Cognitive Dissonance California: Stanford University Press

2. Pink, D. (2009) Drive: the surprising truth about what motivates us' Riverhead

CHAPTER 3

Habits

Strengthening our intentions and acting purposefully

We've looked at the need to have a purpose and instil a purpose in others. We've seen the importance of vision and the need to not only have our own vision, but also to empower those we lead to have their own vision. However, just having vision and finding meaning isn't enough. We also need to do something with it. Have you ever had a great vision, but deep down had a thought along the lines of: 'I know me, I know I can't achieve that' or even 'I've had big visions before but they never come off'?

To achieve the visions we have we need to move beyond 'knowing me as I am' to 'knowing who I could be if I lived purposefully'. It is a subtle difference but very important.

This chapter looks at creating a culture that is purposeful and focused on achieving what we want to achieve. It is different from the culture of meaning that the previous chapter looks at. That chapter is about having a purpose in your life; this one is about how to achieve that purpose.

The focus of this chapter is our habits. Our habits are powerful and have a large impact on us emotionally and physically. We will look at identifying what our habits are and then creating strategies for breaking them and developing a more purposeful behaviour.

The aim is to create a culture, individually for you as a leader, and within your organisations that recognises the power of habits, identifies unhealthy habits, breaks unhealthy habits and replaces them with new, purposeful behaviours.

The impact of doing this is enormous. As you go through this chapter I encourage you to spend time reflecting and putting new personal strategies in place. By taking control of our habits we move towards greater engagement.

Our habits

Have you ever had the best intentions to start doing things differently? It could be many things; getting fit, managing your money better, investing more in relationships with children, spouses or work colleagues. Whatever these intentions have been, how have you done at sticking to them? How often have your intentions smoothly and seamlessly become your normal way of doing things?

If you are anything like me you have struggled badly in this area. I could give you a list of the best intentions I have had that I haven't stuck at. Sometimes I have been incredibly passionate about the intention and yet I still haven't stuck at them. When I was younger sport was my thing, to begin with athletics and then rugby. I was pretty good and played at quite a high level, but the higher I played the more I realised that my natural talent that had got me so far, wasn't enough to take me to the professional levels of the sport. There were many people with far more talent than me, so what I needed to do was put in the hard work, in fact harder work than the others to make up for the difference in talent. I really wanted to do this. I wanted to be a professional rugby player, but when push came to shove, I couldn't stick at this intention. My habit, of training and working to an average level, was stronger than my intention of working harder than everyone else. After a few weeks, I found I was doing what I had always done, despite the passion, the vision and the intention.

This phenomenon is not unusual. In fact it is very well researched. Psychologist Trandis[1] led the way with his research looking at why people behave the way they do. He found three high level factors that influence our decisions; our habits, our intentions and the facilitating conditions. What's more interesting is that he found our habits are twice as strong as our intentions and the facilitating conditions put together. So to put that another way; the frequency of what we have done in the past is the single biggest factor that will determine what we do in the future.

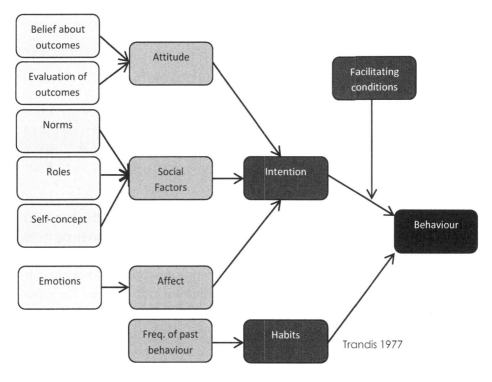

Trandis 1977

Think about this in terms of New Year's resolutions. You decide to get fit so you join the gym. You go religiously for the first week or so. Then you get a cold and miss a session. You have a busy day at work so you miss another. The kids are ill so you miss another and pretty soon you find that you are wasting the exorbitant gym membership you have signed up for and are tied into for another 11 months!

Cialdini, in his studies, identified how routine behaviour becomes detached from the original motivating factors; changing those factors (eg. attitudes or intentions) will not necessarily change the habit, as their power in influencing the behaviour has become weakened[2].

Have you ever been on a training course where you have had a light bulb moment and you've thought; "Yes! That is exactly what I need to start doing to get the best out of my team." You go back to the day job with the best intentions to start doing whatever it was and without even realising it, you carry on doing exactly what you have always done.

Becoming more purposeful

The first stage in doing something about this has to be to identify what habits are holding us back. Some of these might be obvious, but others will be hidden and you may not even be aware of the effect they are having on your life and the way they are stopping you from reaching your potential.

Spend time reflecting on where you feel you are not as effective and purposeful as you could be. Identifying these areas will generally help us to find the habit that is holding us back and reducing our effectiveness. If you are stuck for inspiration and can't identify habits that hold you back, ask your colleagues friends and family. They are sure to help you out!

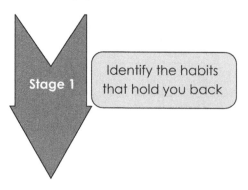

Stage 1 — Identify the habits that hold you back

Bracing our minds

Stage 1 — Identify the habits that hold you back

Stage 2 — 'Brace' your minds against these habits

This concept of 'bracing our minds' is central to a lot of the academic studies that look at how to stop acting habitually. The premise is that we fall back into our old habits, our old behaviours, usually sub-consciously without even realising we are doing it.

'Bracing our mind' acts to increase the power of our intentions so that our habits don't win the war on our behaviour so easily. Remember the work by Trandis written about earlier in the chapter? His findings resulted in the following equation:

Habits = 2 X (intentions + facilitating conditions)

Well if we can strengthen our intentions so we remain conscious of them more often, then we begin to redress this equation.

In the corporate world of executive coaching 'don't do lists' are becoming really popular. Some of you may be the organised type of person who writes 'to do' lists, well this is the opposite. The idea is to write down the habits that you are trying to stop doing and to put that list somewhere visible where you will see it frequently throughout the day. It works particularly well if the list is placed near to where the habit is undertaken, that is if there is a particular geographical location for the habit you are trying to stop. By making your intentions more visible, you increase awareness of what you are trying to do and reduce the chance of subconsciously falling back into the habit.

Refocusing your mind on the vision

Also important is what we focus our minds with and for. We have to go back to the vision that we have. We need to think about what it will be like when we have achieved it, what it will feel like and the sense of achievement we will experience. We need to brace our minds to the vision we have. A brace literally connects you to the thing you are bracing yourself to. We have to connect ourselves so strongly to the vision that other thoughts cannot pull us away from this place.

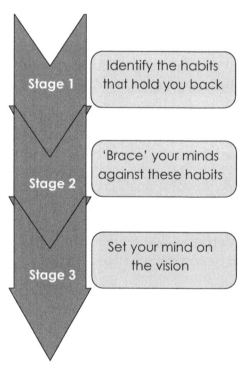

Stage 1 — Identify the habits that hold you back

Stage 2 — 'Brace' your minds against these habits

Stage 3 — Set your mind on the vision

It is important to focus attention on the positive results you will get by behaving differently. This is the premise behind DEEP. It provides facts and figures to show leaders the impact on productivity if they change the way they lead. The hope they gain from knowing this further strengthens their intentions to behave differently and to stick at these new behaviours; bracing themselves to this hope despite many other forces encouraging them to revert to their old ways.

Expectation

Focusing on the vision is an important ingredient in changing habits. Another ingredient is to change the mind-sets we have that limit our behaviour.

We often make assumptions about what is possible and can be expected, usually based on our experiences of how things have gone in the past. This can then limit our behaviour so it then isn't possible to move beyond our previous experiences.

I came across a fascinating example of this recently.

The Iron Curtain was traced by an electrified barbed-wire fence that isolated the communist world from the West.

Deer still balk at crossing the border with Germany even though the physical fence came down a quarter century ago, new studies show.

Czechoslovakia, where the communists took power in 1948, had three parallel electrified fences, patrolled by heavily armed guards. Nearly 500 people were killed when they attempted to escape communism.

Deer were also victims of the barrier. A seven-year study in the Czech Republic's Sumava National Park showed that the original Iron Curtain line still deters one species, red deer, from crossing.

"It was fascinating to realize for the first time that anything like that is possible," said Pavel Sustr, a biologist who led the Czech

project. Scientists conducting research on German territory reached similar conclusions.

The average life expectancy for deer is 15 years and none living now would have encountered the barrier.[3]

The deer alive today have never experienced the electric shock that their ancestors would have done. Yet they still don't cross the border where the fence used to be. They have become so conditioned by their expectations and the expectations passed down to them they can't hope for anything more or anything different.

The same can happen to us. We become so conditioned to our environment, experiences and training that we often don't hope for anything more or anything different. We don't even realise that more is possible or available.

This brings us back to vision. The vision must lift people's eyes up beyond the everyday to something aspirational. It needs to help people see what could be possible. It needs to excite and tantalise people at the possibilities if the vision is realised. It could be about growth, customer service or something else. The key is that the vision takes people beyond current performance and experience and gives them a glimpse of what is possible.

How do we sustain it?

Developing new purposeful behaviours and tackling habitual behaviours and patterns of thinking, is not a one off event. We need to constantly be checking ourselves and tackling thinking and behaviours that are not helping us to achieve our vision. When we do the result is dramatic. We experience a greater level of engagement because we actually have greater peace as our satisfaction with our self is actually increased. The time it takes for us to change a new behaviour into a habit depends on the type of behaviour; whether it is health and fitness related, to do with the way we think or something else. However there seems to be a magic time period for changing habits and creating new behaviours of somewhere between four and twelve weeks. If we can stick at our new behaviours for this time period then they become our new habits and influence our future behaviour.

The Role of Other People

As Trandis' equation has shown us there are two factors that can help to outweigh the power of our habits. They are our intentions and the facilitating conditions. We've already looked at increasing the power of our intentions by 'bracing our minds'. The other aspect to look at is increasing the power of the facilitating conditions.

A lot of the successes people have had in changing culture in organisations at a corporate level have been in creating 'peer accountability networks' within the workplace. This is a great example of awful management speak, but the essence that underpins it is good.

When trying to introduce new behaviours, or break old habits, making people more aware is very important. If a whole group of people are supporting each other in making this change, then this drastically improves the strength of the 'facilitating conditions'.

Peer accountability networks are just groups of people who have all given each other permission to hold each other to account when they spot one of them behaving in a way they are trying to change. In fact they are often even more proactive than that, they regularly ask people how they are doing at ....., whatever it might be.

When this works best it isn't heavy or judgemental. It is a group of people, often in a very light-hearted way, reminding each other of what they are trying to do and what the result will be if they manage it. It is often a bit 'sticky' at first because we are such private people. However I find it works. It makes people realise they are not in it alone and that together, they can crack it, whatever 'it' is. It brings the secret personal battles into the open so that the community supports each person to achieve their goals. It transforms the 'facilitating conditions' and topples the scales on Trandis' equation.

Creating a Culture in your organisation

Habits are important and getting a grip on them is vital to engagement. It is important that we do this personally as leaders, but it still leaves the question; how do I create a culture within my organisation that gets a grip on habits so that individually and corporately we have increased engagement?

The following are my ideas for doing this:

1.) Involve colleagues from across the organisation to identify habits, both in terms of behaviour and thinking, which limit what is possible in the organisation. These could be personal or 'corporate habits'.

2.) Get an understanding of what could be possible if these habits weren't there and were replaced with positive ones. When possible combine facts, figures and numbers with stories. This is where 'best practice' and case studies from other organisations similar to yours can be useful. Another useful starting point is to reflect on times when the organisation has worked really well and delivered above expectations. What are the characteristics of this time? What did it feel like for those involved? From these points of success imagine what it would be like if these were the norm. What would it be like if the high points that you have experienced were the everyday way of working. What would you achieve and what would it be like for each individual involved.

3.) Create a strong and compelling vision through this process. This should be done through involvement with as many people as possible. The aim of the vision is twofold; to create dissatisfaction personally and corporately with the current state and to show what the future could look like.

4.) Strengthen hope by continually sharing stories of how you are moving towards the vision. Over time it becomes normal and expected that you are heading towards the vision. Over time the vision becomes more realistic and achievable in people's minds. This increases motivation to play their part in achieving it.

5.) Create the environment for the culture change by equipping each individual to 'increase their intentions' and as groups strengthen the 'facilitating conditions'. This is done by helping each individual personalise the corporate culture change down to their individual habits and behaviours and then creating peer accountability networks so that people support and encourage each other to stick with the new behaviours.

6.) Ensure staff 'dwell' in the vision. Consistently and constantly communicate the vision and the associated new behaviours. In direct marketing there are three key words that are used to ensure campaigns are effective. They are; recency, frequency and potency. If a prospect has seen your message recently, they are far more likely to take action. If they hear the message frequently, they are also more likely to take action and if the message is potent to them it again increases the chances they will take action. The same applies to the leader's communication during this period. The chances that people buy into the vision and into the habitual changes that are necessary are increased if hearing about it is recent, frequent and potent. Potency is created through a very personal approach to leadership. When the leader works with staff to create peer accountability networks, when they are visible and their communication is transparent, then the message is more authentic and potent. This is dealt with more in the chapter on the personal characteristics of leaders.

References

1. Trandis, H 1977. *Interpersonal Behaviour*. Monterey, CA: Brooks/Cole.

2. Cited in Maio, G, B Verplanken, A Manstead, W Stroebe, C Abraham, P Sheeran and M Conner 2007. Social Psychological Factors in Lifestyle Change and Their Relevance to Policy. *Journal of Social Issues and Policy Review*, 1 (1) 99-137

3. http://www.huffingtonpost.com/2014/04/23/deer-iron-curtain_n_5200163.html

CHAPTER 4

Influences

Creating culture not conforming

Early on in my career I worked for a company that wasn't a happy place. It was going through a large change and there was a lot of internal politics and jostling for power. The result of this was a culture of negativity that spread like a cancer. Groups of staff couldn't have a normal conversation without talking about certain key issues. Everyone had an opinion, these opinions differed but the result was negativity, pessimism and ultimately depression.

I enjoyed work, was very ambitious and consciously decided to distance myself from these unhealthy dynamics. However, without realizing, it affected me badly. I never really joined in the negative talk, but the environment sapped the life out of me, took any joy out of the work and made me look for a quick exit! The culture of the workplace had affected me. It had influenced my outlook on life and was robbing me of my chance to live life to the full.

At about the same time my wife and I were living in a unique community in rural Norfolk. It was a converted Victorian workhouse that now consisted of 37 houses and flats. It was located outside the main village in its own grounds and was really very isolated with fields as far as the eye could see in all directions. When we arrived, there was a degree of community life and spirit, but with the normal neighbourly disputes thrown in for good measure. Our house was situated next to one of the communal garden areas and, largely due to my wife's sociable nature; it quickly became a hub for 'community bonding'.

Over the time we were there this community became incredibly strong and shared most things. Most evenings in the summer different groups of neighbours would have a bbq or drinks and there were regular parties. The community really became family.

It wasn't all down to us, but my wife particularly was the catalyst. The way she acted in this community became a model that influenced others and as a result, a family emerged. We moved house after living there for seven years as our family grew. We hated moving, but just couldn't fit into the house anymore. It was such a wrench but we visit frequently and have many close friends there still.

These two stories demonstrate how we are influenced by culture and by others. One story demonstrates how I was influenced very negatively and the other shows how we, as a family, helped to have a positive influence to change a whole community.

The fact is we are influenced by other people. Realising this is important to understanding why we make the decisions we do and behave the way we behave. More important however, is learning how to control the impact influences have on us and how to develop a culture within our organisations that develops and nurtures through generating positive influences. When we do this we start the journey of engagement.

This chapter explores how we are influenced, what we can do about it and how we can turn round cultures so they are positive influences. It will also look at what to do if you are stuck in the middle of a negative culture.

What influences us?

We are influenced by others on a variety of levels. The highest level is the culture that exists in the communities we are part of. As culture changes it influences us. One example of this is the way elders in society are viewed and how this has changed over time. I'm not using this example to make a point about honouring our elders, although it could easily be used to do that, but merely to look at how changes in culture influence us and our behaviours.

When my parents were children they addressed other adults as 'Sir' or 'Madam'. When I was a child I addressed other adults as 'Mr Smith' or 'Mrs Jones'. My children address other adults by their Christian names, as do the vast majority of other children. The expectation society has on the way adults are addressed over these three generations has changed and the last three generations of my family has adapted to this change. My family has been influenced by culture changing and followed suit.

At a different level we are influenced by patterns and trends in culture. Fashion and hairstyles are good examples of this. When I was a teenager, a centre parting, long curtains and an undercut were all the style. I followed this style and have many embarrassing photos to remind me! Looking around today I can't see any young people with a haircut like that, probably just as well!

When I was a teenager, with my curtains and undercut, my Dad got a white Ford Sierra with a spoiler on the back. I thought it was the best car going and loved arriving to school or to friends' houses in it. Fast forward a few years and white became such an unpopular colour for a car that if you were buying a second hand car and had a choice between a white one and pretty much any other colour, the white one would have been considerably less expensive because the colour was so unpopular. Nowadays white cars are en vogue again and represent a large percentage of new car sales. As these trends and patterns change over time, we are influenced by them and follow suit.

The third level of culture we are influenced by is the culture of the groups that we belong to. This includes the organisations and the extended families we are part of. If you think about your family and compare it to other families you know, I'm sure you can pick out some pretty large cultural differences. This becomes particularly obvious when it comes to marriage and then is highlighted further when the first baby comes along and the cultures of parenting you were used to suddenly become so important even though you vowed as a child to never do the same to your kids!

We are influenced by culture. To understand how this impacts on engagement we need to dig a bit deeper to understand how and why it influences us in the way that it does. Psychologists Tajfel and Turner demonstrated that we find our social identity from the groups that we are part of[1]. They found we strongly favour people in the groups that we are in, even if those groups don't represent anything and people have just been randomly assigned to them. So just being part of a group, whether or not we like the others in the group, agree with what it stands for, or do anything in the group, creates an allegiance to it. This means that the groups we are part of, both formal and informal have a strong influencing affect over us.

The fourth level of cultural influence is the people you spend the most time with. Psychologist, Albert Bandura, showed that people learn by observing what others do[2]. He found that we copy the behaviours of others. If the behaviour is good and positive then this can be a positive trait. If it is negative behaviour then the impact on us is also negative.

Cialdini built on this research to show that we actually look to others to see how to behave, especially in; ambiguous situations that we haven't encountered before and in crisis and when we perceive others to be experts[3]. In his original experiment he had some accomplices stare upwards on a street pavement as if they were looking at something although there was actually nothing there! Other people quickly joined them and a large group formed and stayed there long after the accomplices actually left.

I'm sure you've experienced going to an event for the first time and you consciously look at how other people are behaving and, what they are doing, becomes your guide for the way you should behave. A few years ago our company won a contract in Abu Dhabi. The consultants we sent out there all had a thorough briefing on the main cultural differences that impacted on the work they were doing before they left. Despite this, whenever we sent a consultant over there they made sure they stuck closely to someone that had been over there a while and carefully observed and copied everything they did.

All of these influences; culture, group and individual could influence us for good, for bad or it could be neutral. The point is that they do influence us and it is important to understand how and why so we can control the impact.

Reflect on the different forms of influences I've mentioned so far:

- The groups you are in
- Experts
- When we are in crisis
- When in ambiguous situations
- People we like
- People with power over us
- Culture at societal levels, organisations level and extended family level

How do these different areas and groups influence you?   How positive or negative are the influences?

Emotions, action, behaviour.

Imagine that something happens to you, let's keep it simple for the moment and say that, 'the something', is a senior colleague ignores you and doesn't talk to you. This event will affect your emotions and make you feel a certain way.   This in turn will impact on your behaviour and actions.

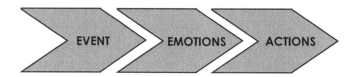

However the process isn't actually as simple as this. There is a stage missing. An event occurring doesn't just impact on our emotions. It impacts on our emotions based on our interpretation of the event. Our mind is critical to the way we react to situations.

Let me give you an example: imagine you are at a conference and you really want to talk to the main speaker. You have read all of their books and love everything they say. It's a lunch break and you see the main speaker near you speaking to someone else. You decide to pluck up the courage to go and speak to them so you 'hover' near them waiting for him to finish their conversation. You know what it's like, you feel uncomfortable and awkward so you try and look natural and busy, perhaps checking your phone for that important message or looking across the room pretending you are trying to see someone else and you aren't really waiting next to the speaker ready to pounce!

You are standing just to the right of the speaker and they finish their conversation. They seem to look right past you, don't notice you, look to their left, see someone else and start talking to them.

This is 'the event', you were waiting to talk to the speaker, they don't notice you and they talk to someone else.

You could interpret this event a number of ways and it is this interpretation that will result in different emotions. You could interpret it as follows:

"I don't believe it. He doesn't want to speak with me. He saw me but just didn't want to speak with me. I don't blame him really, not many people want to speak with me. In fact no-one does really. There isn't much about me that would make people want to speak with me. I'm completely uninteresting, struggle for conversation, I always seem to bore people and man I'm so ugly he probably saw me out of the side of his head and decided to steer clear."

This interpretation of the event would lead to emotions of depression, lack of self-worth and possibly worse!

These emotions would in turn lead to a specific set of behaviours, most likely withdrawal, sitting by yourself and losing any motivation to speak with anyone.

Exactly the same event could be interpreted completely differently:

"Would you believe it? I was standing on his right and he looked to the left and saw someone he knew. What are the chances of that!

This would lead to a whole new set of emotions; possibly increased determination and motivation to be more obvious so he doesn't 'slip through the net' next time. In turn the behaviours and actions could even involve doing star jumps right in front of the speaker so you definitely won't be overlooked next time. It could ultimately lead to a restraining order, but that's another issue!

So it isn't the event itself that impacts on our emotions and actions, but the combination of the event and the way we interpret it in our mind.

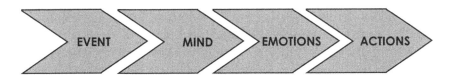

EVENT MIND EMOTIONS ACTIONS

It is the same when looking at the way people and culture influence us. The people and the culture themselves aren't the only factors that lead to changes in our emotions and behaviour, but the combination of the people, culture and our interpretation. This means, to really understand how to get to grips with the way we are influenced personally and to ensure influences within our organisations are positive, we need to look at both what is influencing us and our reaction and interpretation of it.

How is culture influencing us?

So the influences we are under, through the people we spend the most time with and the cultures we are in, impact on us and change us. This can be positive or negative but understanding it is important to engagement.

It is normally easier to think about the way individual people influence us; looking at how culture impacts on us can be much trickier as it is more subtle and can tap into such deeply held beliefs that we don't realise there is another way of thinking or acting.

Take the example of Joan of Arc. French culture had two deeply held assumptions at that time that completely influenced governmental decision making and life in general for the vast majority of French people. They were; that the English could never be beaten and that women could never do anything meaningful.

These paradigms of thinking were so deep that it wasn't talked about, it was just accepted and thoughts and actions came from a place of acceptance rather than questioning and challenging to see if it is true and if there is a different way to think.

It took a maverick, who was ultimately killed for being so radical, to challenge the paradigm and change the culture of France. It was because of Joan of Arc that the French finally realised the English could be beaten. Eventually foreign and military policy changed and as a result the French gained freedom.

All organisations and groups have such paradigms. The unwritten and, often not thought about, assumptions that influence us and guide the way we act.

What deeply held assumptions influence you?

To really understand what forms and reinforces the culture of your organisations, and therefore what is influencing us, it is necessary to look a bit deeper. A useful model for doing this is the cultural web developed by Johnson & Scholes[4]. This helps to identify what is creating and reinforcing the assumptions or paradigm that sits at the heart of the culture you are in. It does this by breaking it down into six different aspects.

The six aspects are:

Stories – not the formal communiques, but the informal stories that members of the group or organisation talk about in private.
- What core beliefs do stories reflect?
- How persuasive are these beliefs (through levels)?
- Do stories relate to:
  - Strengths or weaknesses?
  - Success or failure?
  - Conformity or mavericks?
- Who are the heroes and villains?
- What norms do the mavericks deviate from?

Routines and rituals of members of the group

- Which routines are emphasised?
- Which would look odd if changed?
- What behaviour do routines encourage?
- What are the key rituals?
- What core beliefs do they reflect?
- What do training programmes emphasise?
- How easy are rituals/routines to change?

Organisational structures of the group

- How mechanistic/organic are the structures?
- How flat/hierarchical are the structures?
- How formal/informal are the structures?
- Do structures encourage collaboration or competition?
- What types of power structure do they support?

Control systems of the group

- What is most closely monitored/controlled?
- Is emphasis on reward or punishment?
- Are controls related to history or current strategies?
- Are there many/few controls?

Power structures of the group

- What are the core beliefs of the leadership?
- How strongly held are these beliefs (idealists or pragmatists)?
- How is power distributed in the organisation?
- Where are the main blockages to change?

Symbols of the group

- What language and jargon are used?
- How internal or accessible are they?
- What aspects of strategy are highlighted in publicity?
- What status symbols are there?
- Are there particular symbols which denote the organisation?

This model applies to all organisations we are part of and the groups and friends that we associate ourselves with. The following table identifies the different cultural elements for two businesses that I have worked with. Both of these businesses are successful but look at some of the main cultural differences and imagine how these different cultures would affect you if you were part of the business.

	Business 1	Business 2
Stories	Leaders don't understand Overworked and under paid Not like it used to be	Success and elite level performance Funding reducing but maintaining quality
Symbols	Plush HQ separate from frontline Uniformed staff Liveried vehicles	Support from celebrities
Power	Fragmented Hierarchical leaders Politicians Unions	Centralised but also political for those with 'connections'
Organisational Structures	Hierarchical Mechanistic	Flat
Controls	Centrally set targets Funding linked to achievement of targets	Some set from different funders but quality and achievement of internal targets most important
Routines and Rituals	Shift patterns	Events and informal celebrations after major events

The culture that exists in these businesses impacts on the staff for good and for bad. It impacts on the way they make decisions, what they view as important and ultimately how they see themselves in relation to the vision of the organisation.

Have a go at creating your own cultural webs for your organisation and teams. Break the culture down to identify what is creating and reinforcing it. What are the influences that are not only forming the culture, but are also influencing you? What can you do about them?

The following story shows how small changes in the stories that are told in an organisation, can change the culture and the underpinning paradigm.

The new CEO recognised there was a negative culture pervading the organisation and realised success depended upon doing something about it. He realised that the 'stories' that were told in the organisation were largely negative and that a 'glass half empty' philosophy dominated the business. He decided to change this by introducing a new approach that he started informally by modelling it himself before initiating it as company policy. He did this by simply starting every meeting with a good news story of something good that has happened in the company in the last week.

As good news became a more spoken about topic, he found that over about six months it eroded the power of the negative culture that existed. People began to think of 'what had gone well' ready for the next meeting they had to go to. The act of thinking differently, of allowing positive stories to influence them, made them change their outlook and actually be more positive.

The culture we are in influences us, so we have a responsibility to ensure the culture that is influencing us is as positive as possible. As leaders we have the responsibility to change the culture of our organisations so that it is positive for the people who are working for us. By doing so, the organisation will also achieve its purpose far more effectively and individuals will be engaged.

References

1. Tajfel H and Turner , J (1986) The Social Identity theory of inter-group behaviour' in S. Worchel and L.W. Austin (eds) *Psychology of Intergroup Relations* (Chicago, Nelson-Hall)

2. Bandura A (1977) *Social Learning Theory* Englewood Cliffs, NJ: Prentice Hall

3. Cialdini R (1993) *Influence: Science and Practice* (3rd edn), New York, Harper Collins

4. Johnson and Scholes (2002) *Exploring Corporate Strategy,* Prentice Hall, London

CHAPTER 5

Self-Expectations

Understanding who we are and what we can achieve

We need to have a vision, a purpose for what we are doing and to act purposefully so we see that vision come to life. We also need to understand the way we are influenced by the cultures we are in and the people we spend time with. With this in place we can continue with our purposeful pursuit of our vision and to lead others into their vision.

The next part of the jigsaw is to ensure we have healthy expectations of what we are able to do. Having right expectations is so important to achieving our vision. Many studies prove this to be true; people who achieve are usually those who expect to achieve. So what do healthy expectations look like? How do we develop them and how can we lead others in a way so they also have healthy expectations of themselves?

There are a number of different facets to developing healthy expectations. Two important ones are our self-efficacy and our self-discrepancy.

Identity

Higgins' self-discrepancy theory[1] suggests that at any one point in time we have three views of our self: who we think we are, who we think we should be and who we think other people think we are. When there is a disconnect between these different views it is likely that we start becoming hard on ourselves, negative self-talk begins and ultimately we become depressed and lose engagement and motivation.

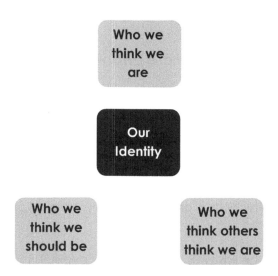

The way we think of ourselves and perceive what others think of us can be mine field.

- If our view of 'who we are' is warped then it is likely to create a disconnect between 'who we think we are' and 'who we think we should be'.

- If our view of 'who we think we should be' is warped then it is likely to also create this same disconnect

- If our view of what others think about us is warped or even that we worry about this when we shouldn't, then it will create a disconnect between 'who we think we are' and 'who we think other people think we are'.

It is really important that we, as leaders, are secure in our identity and model a healthy internal dialogue that flows from this security. The culture we live in is actively fighting against us having a right and balanced view of who we are, who we should be and what others think of us. Culture teaches us to worry about what others think of us, to put on a front and, to some extent, actively try and create a disconnect between these three areas of our thoughts because; 'what people think is more important than the reality'. We need to model a healthy identity to those in our workforces because, in so doing, we release them to also know their identity.

Who do we think we are?

Self-efficacy, understanding what we are able to achieve and not limiting that through unhealthy expectations, is deeply rooted in the view we have of our self. Look through the table on the following page and identify where you have a positive view of yourself and where you don't.

Unhealthy mind set	ISSUE	Healthy mind set
Independent / Self-reliant	**DEPENDENCY**	Interdependent/Acknowledge need
Strive for praise, approval and acceptance	**NEED FOR APPROVAL**	Self-confident and doesn't need others'approval
A need for personal achievement as you seek to impress others, or no motivation to achieve at all	**MOTIVE FOR ACHIEVEMENT**	Achievement is motivated by a deep gratitude of what is already had and a sense of what else could be
Self-rejection from comparing yourself to others	**SELF-IMAGE**	Positive and affirmed because you know you have such value
Seek comfort in counterfeit affections: addictions, compulsions, escapism, busyness	**SOURCE OF COMFORT**	Seek times of quietness and solitude to rest
Competition, rivalry, and jealousy towards others' success and position	**PEER RELATIONSHIPS**	Humility and unity as you value others and are able to rejoice in their success
Accusation and exposure in order to make yourself look good by making others look bad	**HANDLING OTHERSFAULTS**	You overlook issues to focus on the good in people
See authority as a source of pain: distrustful towards them and lack a heart attitude and submission	**VIEW OF AUTHORITY**	Respectful, honouring
Guarded and conditional: based upon others' performance as you seek to get your own needs met	**EXPRESSION OF LOVE**	Open, patient, and affectionate as you lay your life and agendas down in order to meet the needs of others

Who do we think we should be?

The culture in which we live is constantly trying to make us dissatisfied with our present circumstances; to want and expect more, in fact to believe that we deserve more. By doing a quick look back over the past few decades it is easy to see the change happening and the impact of it.   Back in the sixties and seventies, if people couldn't afford something they saved up for it, now we buy it on credit and worry about paying it back later. We have all seen the impact this approach has had on society at large over the last six or seven years!

It can be hard to live in the now and find contentment with who we are and what we are doing now. However, living in the present and being present is so important.   That isn't to say having vision and ambition is bad, far from it. What isn't healthy though, is having such a focus on the future that we lose peace and contentment with who we are today and we put off doing what we should do today because we are waiting for tomorrow.

The more we allow this culture of dissatisfaction and entitlement to influence us, the greater the disconnect we create between who we are and who we think we should be.

What do others think about us?

The final part of Higgins' self-discrepancy theory is worrying about what others think of us. If we perceive a difference between who we think they think we are and who we think we are, then we can become negative towards ourselves. We need to worry less about other people and focus on what is right.

Thinking about, worrying about and acting based on what others think of us is not sustainable and will not lead us and others into engagement.

We need to demonstrate, in our leadership, how to respect others, but not be driven by looking for their approval or respect. We need to be people of purpose who know what is right and stick to that course. That isn't to say we become dictators and don't take others' views into account. What I mean is we aren't swayed by what they think about us personally.

Authority

Bandura's theory of self-efficacy[2] suggests that we limit ourselves by our own expectations. To put it simply; if we don't think we can achieve something then we are very unlikely to achieve it. I think it is perhaps easier to reflect on when the opposite is true, when we have a real deep down assurance we are going to succeed in something and that then comes to pass.

I particularly notice this phenomenon when playing golf, or rather trying badly to play golf. I stand at the ball with my club ready and I know before I swing the club whether it will be a good shot or whether I will fluff it. Why I know, I'm not sure. It could be because I am subconsciously working out whether I am standing correctly. It could be that actually the only thing that affects the shot is the thought in my head! If I think it will be a good shot, I relax and it generally is. If I think it will be a bad shot, I tense up and swing wrong. I don't know the reason, but I know it happens on multiple occasions when playing a round of golf. The more disconcerting thing is I still don't learn to stop the shot and start again when I do get these feelings!

A large amount of sports psychology is focused in this area; helping sports people believe that they have got what it takes to perform at the level required. In the work place the same phenomena is also very evident. People who 'make it' in work, whatever that means, are seldom those who don't know how they did and never thought they would. People who rise to the top in work, sports and other areas of life are usually those who have a deep self confidence in who they are and the ability that they have.

An interesting study has been done looking at young ice hockey players in Canada[3]. The study conclusively proved that children who had a birthday early in the school year are statistically far more likely to become a professional hockey player. The reason for this is as they are growing up they are the older kids in the year and therefore normally bigger than those whose birthday is later in the year. Size matters in hockey so in these early, formative years as a hockey player, they outperform those who are younger than them. Over time the physical difference disappears, but the self-confidence born from having out performed others remains. This results in a far higher proportion of those born early in the school year, becoming professional in comparison to those born later in the school year.

Balancing Expectations

In the work I have done in large organisations there seems to be a tipping point for leading other people's expectations. If we expect too much of them we overwhelm them and decrease their engagement. However, often we hold people back; we don't allow them to flourish or use their strengths and giftings and as a result, their self-expectations are greater than their ability to use their strengths and giftings. This also decreases engagement.

As leaders we have to find the tipping point. We need to push people who need pushing beyond their expectations, whilst supporting them. We also need to develop character in others whilst empowering them towards their expectations.

References

1. Higgins, E.T. (1987) Self-discrepancy: A theory relating self and affect. Psychological Review, 94, 319-340

2. Bandura, A. (1977) Self-efficacy: Toward a unifying theory of behaviour change, Psychological Review, 84(2), 191-215

3. http://www.plosone.org/article/info%3Adoi%2F10.1371%2Fjournal.pone.0057753

CHAPTER 6

LOSS

How fear, risk and loss aversion impact on our thinking

I've worked on and been involved in many change projects. They rarely seem to go smoothly as they are times of such heightened emotions. There was a particular project I was working on in which I came across a lady called Jeanette. She worked for an NHS Trust that was going through a fairly major change and reorganisation programme. She was a junior manager and had understood the need for the change and the logic and rationale behind the way it was being done. However she couldn't get her heart around it even though she understood it in her head.

After spending some time with her it emerged there were two main issues: the fact that what she was losing in the process, or that she perceived she was losing, was more important to her than the benefits of the programme. Secondly, the uncertainty that the change created was very unsettling for her. She was losing a support network of people she had grown to know and trust. As part of the change she was moving to a different part of the building to work with people she didn't know too well. It was probably a good opportunity for her, with greater career prospects and she knew that. However, it seemed the logical, rational benefits were outweighed by the sense of loss she was also experiencing.

To engage others we need to understand how and why people respond to change in the way they do and in fact we need to understand why we respond in the way that we do!

This chapter looks at loss and fear because they are actually dealing with the same issue.   Our fear is often based on our assessment of the risks involved and what we stand to gain and loose.   Jeanette was affected by the loss of the team she was working with because she feared she wouldn't create the same level of trusting relationship with the new team she would be working with.

Kahneman and Tversky pioneered a particularly psychological theory called Prospect Theory[1] that has since been the subject of many rigorous studies.   Their findings have withstood the test of these studies and give us some interesting insights into the way humans work.   The main principles behind prospect theory are:

Certainty: People have a strong preference for certainty and are willing to sacrifice potential gain to achieve more certainty. For example, if option A is a guaranteed win of £1,000, and option B is an 80 percent chance of winning £1,400 but a 20 percent chance of winning nothing, people tend to prefer option A.

Loss aversion: People tend to give losses more weight than gains — they're loss averse. So, if you gain £100 and lose £80, it may be considered a net *loss* in terms of satisfaction, even though you came out £20 ahead, because you'll tend to focus on how much you lost, not on how much you gained.

Understanding our desire for certainty, the fact we are loss averse and the impact fear has on us, gives us further clues about engaging others in a meaning full way that increases productivity.

Certainty

Consistency and certainty are strong driving forces in us humans. We want to know where we stand financially, in our relationships and in our work. Society is structured around having this kind of consistency and certainty. Most of us have a regular monthly salary that is needed to pay the regular monthly mortgage and other regular monthly bills. We budget based on our regular monthly income and outgoings. We hope for security in our jobs so that we can commit to these regular monthly commitments. We look to give certainty and consistency for our children by not moving around too much so they can stay in the same school etc.

None of this is wrong and in fact, more often than not, is based on good wisdom and is an example of good stewardship of the things we have been given; money, resources and a family. However, it is also important to see it for what it is; a strong psychological desire to base our decision making on certainty rather than risk.

We make conservative decisions because the need for certainty is hard wired into our thinking. I am obviously generalising here and there are many people who buck this trend, however, for the majority of the population, this is how we think.

Whilst there is much wisdom and good stewardship that comes from this way of thinking, it also creates major problems when trying to change; individually and in workplaces. The reason it creates these problems is because our certainty is based largely on our experiences and therefore doesn't allow for new experiences with different results.

One of the most common factors that we come up against when trying to help implement a programme of change, is that people have already made up their mind about whether a programme of change is a good thing or not. This position is largely created from their experiences of previous change programmes, either in their current organisation or in past ones. These experiences create expectations, both for the programme overall, and for the individual's own reaction to the change programme. As we have seen in the chapter on self-expectations, this sets the limit to their expected experience of the current change programme. Put simply, if someone thinks the change is rubbish, will be done badly and affect them emotionally, that is probably the way they will relate to the change programme because that is their expectation of it from the beginning.

In many businesses people have been so hurt by their previous experiences of change that the mere thought of it conjures up such powerful emotions that are far stronger than rational thought and decision making.

One of the most interesting parts of the example of certainty given at the beginning of this chapter is the perceived chance of winning nothing. In the example there was the chance of turning £1,000 into £1,400 but there was also a 20% chance of winning nothing. The percentage chance of winning nothing, or losing, is a judgement call we make and is coloured by our experiences. For example someone could think "my experience of the last change I went through was that it was done badly so I think the chance of winning nothing is 50% not 20%". Our perception of winning nothing, of being affected badly, is based on a judgement call that comes from our experiences.

The same is true when thinking about taking risks in business. The percentage chance of 'winning nothing' is largely based on our previous experiences and self-expectations. For example I could think; "I won't call that company to try and make a sale because my experience tells me that my chance of 'not winning' and them not buying is high, so despite the fact it would be amazing if it did happen, I'm not going to do it. What's more I'm not sure I could deal with the rejection of them saying no."

Does this pattern of thinking sound familiar? We perceive two areas of loss in this equation: firstly that the sale won't happen and secondly that our emotions will be negatively impacted. This perception of loss reduces our perceived chance of winning and increases the attractiveness of maintaining the status quo and not stepping out and taking a risk.

The same goes for our attitude towards having difficult conversations with staff or managers or indeed anything else where we perceive there to be an element of risk.

The subconscious decision making process we go through tells us that the certainty we have in doing things the way we have always done them, is stronger than the potential increase we will get by taking a risk.

Other research undertaken suggests that the potential gain has to be twice that of the potential loss for people to consider the risk worth taking. In the experiment people were given a 50/50 chance of either winning or losing money. People would only take that chance if the amount they might win was worth twice the value of what they might lose.

Loss Aversion

The other part of Prospect Theory, loss aversion, is interesting as it provides another insight into human nature. An interesting experiment was done in London's Spitalfields Market by the BBC programme Horizon. Strangers were approached and given £20 and offered the chance to increase that to £50 by betting it against a roulette wheel.

This was the basic scenario, but it was put to people in two different ways. In the first scenario people were given £20 and told they could stick with the £20 or they could use it to bet and possibly turn it into £50. The vast majority of people approached using this method, stuck with the £20.

The second way people were approached was slightly different. They were given £50 and immediately had £30 taken away. They were told they could win it back by betting the £20 they still had. Looking at this rationally it is the same scenario. People ended up with £20 they didn't have before and were told they could either keep it or use it to gamble with to possibly gain another £30.

However, because of the different way the scenario was put to the people, the results were totally different. One group had the full £50 in their hands to begin with, so when £30 was taken away from them they felt they had lost something. The majority of people approached using this scenario decided to gamble the money compared to a very small percentage of people using the other scenario.

Most people are more concerned about keeping what they've got than gaining something they have never had. We worry more about loss than gain. As leaders we must be aware of this in ourselves so we don't pass opportunities over. We also must be aware of this in the way we lead our people.

Fear

There are many potential sources of fear for a leader: a lack of self-confidence, imposter syndrome (feeling that you are a fake and blagging it), a culture in your work environment of coming down hard on failure, tough market conditions that make every decision vital, a worry for the future or worry of what others will think of you. A good staging post for dealing with fear is to focus on stopping the symptoms of fear affecting our leadership.

By focusing on stopping the symptoms of fear we will, over time, change our habitual way of thinking and reduce the impact of fear on our leadership.

The symptoms of fearful leadership

We disempower others as our power decreases - the leader takes more and more upon their own shoulders as they don't trust others to achieve the same results they could or because they feel threatened by gifted people in their workplaces. This decreases engagement by reducing involvement and autonomy. Empowering others to use and develop their gifts and strengths and involving others in key decisions are all motivating factors that increase engagement in workforces and, in so doing, move people towards engagement. Giving others autonomy is also proven to be a highly motivating factor whilst disempowering staff reduces their involvement and autonomy. One of the personal characteristics of engaging leaders is that they are trustworthy and they trust others. The likelihood is that trust is also undermined by disempowering others.

The strength of relationships decrease as our love decreases – when the leader draws everything closer to themselves and are less trusting and authentic in their relationships, it decreases engagement by reducing trust in the relationships and changing the values of the relationship. Trust is again the main characteristic that will be eroded by succumbing to fear in leadership. Followers will feel they aren't trusted and in turn the trust they have in their leader will decrease. A change in the strength of relationship says quite a bit about the values, particularly the informal values that are evident in the workplace. When we see alignment between our personal values and the formal and informal values of the workplace we are more engaged and more a part of it. The converse is also true!

The quality of decisions decreases as our self-control decreases - the leader's emotional intelligence is reduced and they have less awareness of the impact they have on others, less empathy with others and less self-control. This decreases engagement by reducing trust and hope. We also become less stable in the way we respond to people as our self-control is reduced, which again decreases their engagement and connection.   When emotional intelligence is reduced, our ability to control our self is also reduced, leading to instability. Hope and compassion; two other important characteristics of engaging leaders also decrease as fear affects decision making.

The Impact of fearful leadership

An obvious impact on people when fear becomes a part of our decision making is a reduction in engagement and connection. This becomes a vicious cycle; as fear increases, connection drops further which reinforces this unhealthy loop. The less obvious impact is that we never become the leader we could be. We don't reach our potential and have the impact we could have because we are hamstrung by fear affecting our thinking.

The opposite of fear based leadership is empowering leadership based on good relationships and high emotional intelligence. To have power and be powerful is to give it away and empower others. To demonstrate love in the workplace is to build good relationships. Self-control or high levels of emotional intelligence have been shown by Daniel Goleman to be the main distinguishing factor that separates great leaders with average leaders[2]. Staff not being empowered by defensive leaders, relationships breaking down and leaders who lack self-control and awareness of the impact they have on others, are three of the most common problems I see across businesses of all types and are some of the main reasons for low levels of engagement. The root of this is fear.

To be engaged and to engage others we must recognise that there are some patterns of thought that are natural to us which are actually counter productive to engagement.

The following two check lists are to help you reflect on how loss aversion, the need for certainty and fear affect your thinking and decision making.

References

1.Kahneman, D & Tversky, A. (1979) Prospect Theory: An Analysis of Decision Under Risk. Econometrica. XLVII: 263-291

2. Goleman, D. (1995) Emotional Intelligence, why it matters more than IQ

Personal check list

		Yes	No
1	Do you perceive the future based on your past experiences?		
3	Is the value you are placing on the status quo right and healthy?		
4	Do you see the possibilities?		
5	Is the fear of losing powerful and do you think it is likely you will lose?		
6	Do you focus more on loss or gain?		
7	Is fear masquerading as wisdom?		

Leading other to gain - check list

1	How are past experiences affecting expectations of the future?	
2	How can you increase dissatisfaction with the status quo?	
3	How can you create an empowering culture?	
4	How can you strengthen relationships?	
5	How can you make better decisions through good self-control and increase emotional intelligence across the organisation?	

CHAPTER 7

Personal characteristics

The characteristics that engage

It is easy to see how our personal characteristics effect the engagement of others. The culture we create through our example and the decisions we make have direct consequences in others' lives and therefore impact on their engagement.

The research we have done has found the leadership culture that exists in organisations to be the single biggest factor that impacts on engagement. This means it is also the biggest factor influencing the productivity of the organisation and the quality of life of the employees / members. This culture is set by us, the leaders.

Some really interesting research has been undertaken by Gallup looking at the personal characteristics of leaders that have the most engaged followers. Their premise is that to find out what leadership characteristics engage people, the ones to ask are not the leaders, but the followers of leaders. What is it about their leaders that engages or disengages them?

They conducted this research globally between 2005 and 2008, initially with around 10,000 people, creating a strong and robust research base to draw conclusions from. They asked people to think of a leader that has the most positive effect on their daily life and then to think of what this person contributes to their life[1].

They concluded there are four characteristics that are more important than any others in engaging followers. Engaged followers means two things, firstly that they are enjoying their work; secondly, that they are more productive so the organisation, of whatever type, achieves more.

The four characteristics they found to be so important are; trust, hope, compassion and stability.

Trust

Gallup found the chance of an employee being engaged at work if they don't trust the company's leaders is 1 in 12. However the chances of an employee being engaged if they do trust the company's leaders are better than 1 in 2. This is more than a six fold increase and will have a corresponding impact on productivity, performance and the life that the employee is living.

So what is it that leads to trust or in fact distrust. At a very obvious level if the leader is a liar or found to be unethical in the decisions they make, then trust is eroded. However the picture is actually far more complex than that. I'm sure many of you have worked with leaders who have the best intentions and want to give the best results for their staff. The result of this is they can often over promise. They say they will do things and have the best intentions to do them, but never quite deliver against what they say they will do. This might come from a good place, but actually the effect is the same; trust is eroded.

Stephen M.R. Covey, in his book; The Speed of Trust[2] identifies four key components of trust: integrity, intent, capability and results. The first two are internal factors that others judge us by whilst the second two relate to our performance and whether others will trust us to do a certain task based on their perception of our ability and track record.

Every year Edelman conducts a global study of trust looking at levels of trust in 26 countries in government, business, NGOs and the media[3]. Part of their research involves looking at how much people trust the leaders in these four different spheres of society. To measure this they have created the Edelman Trust Barometer. The Trust Barometer identifies 16 specific attributes which build trust and clusters them into five groups; engagement, integrity, products and services, purpose and operations.

When going through the checklist, a useful question to ask might be; 'how would others score me in these areas'? Try and put yourself in their shoes. If you're really brave, perhaps ask them to score you, but make sure you give them permission to be completely honest and don't get defensive at the results if they are not what you expected!

Score yourself between 1 and 5 for these 16 attributes with 5 being very good and 1 very poor.

Listens to customer needs and feedback

Treats employees well

Places customers ahead of profits

Communicates frequently and honestly on the state of the business

Has ethical business practices

Takes responsible actions to address an issue or crisis

Has transparent and open business practices

Offers high quality products and services

Is an innovator of new products, services or ideas

Works to protect and improve the environment

Addresses societies needs in everyday business issues

Creates programmes that positively impact on the local community

Partners with NGOs, government and 3rd parties to address societal needs

Has highly regarded and widely admired top leadership

Ranks on a global list of top companies

Delivers consistent financial returns to investors

TOTAL

Trust and Culture

It is interesting and useful to look a bit deeper into the Edelman report as it shows some cultural trends in trust that identify some of the barriers we might face as we look to build trust.

Levels of trust vary from country to country, ranging from a score of 80 for China, down to 36 for Russia. The scores reveal, not only the way business is done or perceived to be done in these countries, but also the levels of trust in the different cultures. The culture of trust that exists in a country will have an impact on the levels of trust in your organisation. Individuals are impacted on by the prevailing culture and as a result, view events, organisation and people through the lens of that culture. Both the US and UK come in the middle of the league table of trust. The US scores 59 and the UK 53 although both of the scores are up considerably from the year before.

Hope

Gallup's research found that 69% of employees who feel enthusiastic about the future are engaged in their jobs compared to 1% who are not enthusiastic about the future. Instilling hope in people is a foundational requirement for leading. Hope allows people to see beyond their current circumstances towards something better.

We need to spend time deliberately creating hope for the future and positioning ourselves to also be hopeful. This can be a challenge and in my experience there are two main barriers to doing this:

- Busyness, reacting to the needs of today
- Difficult and uncertain futures

It is difficult to give hope in situations that seem hopeless. Many of our clients have gone through large restructures and cost cutting exercises recently and, as a result, made many people redundant. It is very hard for a manager to give hope in these circumstances and even harder to do it in a genuine and authentic way that doesn't undermine the trust staff have in them. Trust that is very important as we have just read!

Creating and communicating hope for others requires us to be proactive. Hope comes from looking to the future not by responding to the needs of today. Many of us are pretty bad at this and are getting worse. 'Busyness syndrome', as it is being coined, is affecting all walks of life and actually reducing our productivity let alone our ability to convey hope to others.

Busyness syndrome seems to be created from three sources:

1. Finding self-worth through being busy and letting others know how busy we are

2. Poor skills of prioritisation, focusing our time on low priority tasks that are perhaps urgent but not important rather than important tasks that perhaps don't have the same deadlines

3. A culture of now and of distractions - we expect replies quickly, we get messages immediately on our phones and tablets all of which makes it easier to respond to small, less urgent tasks.

Try and identify areas of hopelessness in your business. What is the assumption behind the hopelessness? The following are examples of assumptions I hear all of the time in businesses:

• The market is too hard, the clients just don't spend money any more

• The competition can do this better than we will ever be able to

• This change will go badly because they always do and no one likes change

You get the idea. Identify the hopelessness, then identify the assumption that sits behind the hopelessness and challenge the assumption. Is there are different way of looking at the situation?

Compassion

The most productive companies have a leadership culture that focuses on developing and recognising staff, encouraging open feedback and promoting teamwork.

According to research by Christina Boedker, from the Australian School of Business, out of all of the various measurements they looked at in an organisation, the ability of the leader to be compassionate – that is, *"to understand people's motivators, hopes and difficulties and to create the right support mechanism to allow people to be as good as they can be"* – that had the greatest correlation with profitability and productivity.

The field of research that I am involved in, behavioural economics, is demonstrating quite clearly that the old "command and control" style of leadership is not nearly as effective as a "connect and collaborate" style.

Those that lead by intimidation might appear to get results, but they end up being short-term, often causing anxiety in others. This leads to poor workplace morale and staff who either leave the company prematurely, fail to work at their best or become saboteurs. The same is true if you tone down the word 'intimidation' to, leading by the force of their personality. They could be very nice people who are great fun to work with, but a focus on task as opposed to relationship will not get the same results in the long run.

In the past, a compassionate style of leadership was seen as weak. However demonstrating compassion, whilst still meeting hard targets and objectives, is actually far more challenging than a more autocratic style of leadership.

But what does compassion mean?

When we talk about compassion in the workplace, it is easy to mistake it for letting people get away with things and not having the difficult conversations that need to be had. This isn't compassion at all. Compassion is about making those difficult decisions and tackling poor performance, but with a focus on wanting the best for the person and helping them to become the best that they can be. This sometimes means compassionately letting people go.

Avoiding difficult conversations and letting people get away with things, is actually the opposite of being compassionate as it isn't helping them be their best and is probably also being unfair on others who have to work harder to make up for the performance of those that aren't pulling their weight.

I designed a change programme a few years ago for a large disabled rights charity. They had a policy that they would actively provide employment opportunities for disabled staff, as it was in line with the values of the organisation. However, there was a perception that the disabled staff were allowed to get away with more than the able bodied staff which led to a divide, reduced engagement and ultimately bad relationships and poor performance. The 'compassion' shown to those disabled staff actually back fired as it resulted in a perceived lack of compassion for the able bodied staff.

The following are seven characteristics of compassionate leadership. As you read them try and identify areas that you can work on to become more compassionate.

Listen, listen and listen again- compassionate leaders listen more than they talk. When making tough decisions and facing bad news they don't jump to conclusions but gather more information.

Assume the best in others – a quote I heard recently although I'm not sure where from, is that when thinking of others we judge their behaviour, when thinking of ourselves we judge our motives. We need to judge others as we judge ourselves and see why they are doing what they are doing and what they are trying to achieve.

Keep your emotions in check – We need self-control so that we relate to others as we would plan, not as we would react.

Be interested in others – show that you are genuinely interested in others not just asking questions without really listening. People see through a lack of authenticity so you really do have to be interested in others for them to think you are interested in them!

Accept responsibility - According to Brian Tracy, the motivational guru, the hallmark of a fully mature human being is to be 100% responsible for our lives. Blaming others and creating excuses for our mistakes is one of the primary causes for failure as adults and a contributor to poor mental health[4].

Be open to feedback – feedback shows us the impact of our actions and opens our eyes to things we are not aware off. We must learn to rejoice in feedback, weigh it, accept the useful parts, change things based on useful feedback and not allow feedback to damage us.

Support others in their vision – we must focus on helping each person be the best they can be, whether that is in their career or something else!

Stability

People want to follow someone who provides a solid foundation; it gives them stability to be with other people who provide stability. The stability that people are looking for is largely emotional stability. To receive this we need to know how people will react to situations. I used to work for someone who, when things were going well, was great fun and a joy to work with. When he was stressed, you knew it was time to head for cover as you could see the vein start throbbing on the side of his head and you knew his self-control was reduced. This led to many unhealthy conflict situations and some questionable decision making. The effect across the company was reduced motivation and a work force who didn't really want to be there.

Stability means we are emotionally self-aware, in control of emotional expression, secure, and positive. Many studies have found that emotional intelligence, which includes the characteristics just mentioned, is the biggest determinant as to whether a leader will be successful or not.

What kind of stability do you give those around you? Read the following five statements. Then use a 1-5 (low-high) scale to rate your level of agreement:

___ I have good self-control; I don't get negatively emotional and angry.

___ I perform well under pressure.

___ I'm an optimistic person who sees the positive side of situations.

___ I give people lots of praise and encouragement; I don't put people down and criticise.

___ I view myself as being relaxed and secure, rather than nervous and insecure.

Leading for engagement

Our personal characteristics impact on others. In fact they are a large determinant of the engagement of those in our businesses. We need to be trustworthy and trusting. We need to give hope. We need to be compassionate and we need to be stable and emotionally mature.

By developing these characteristics our staff will be more engaged and in fact we also become more engaged as well.

References

1. Rath, T. & Conchie, B. (2008) Strength Based Leadership, Gallup Press, New York

2. Covey, S (2006) The Speed of Trust, Free Press, New York

3.http://www.edelman.com/insights/intellectual-property/2014-edelman-trust-barometer

4.http://www.digicast.com.au/blog/bid/91694/Why-removing-Personal-Responsibility-is-Irresponsible

CHAPTER 8

Strengths

We are motivated by doing things we are good at

A Gallup study found that when an organisation's leadership fail to focus on individuals' strengths, the odds of an employee being engaged are 1 in 11. But when an organisation's leadership focuses on the strengths of its employees, the odds of them being engaged increase to around 3 in 4. So when we focus on the strengths of those in our businesses they are far more likely to be engaged.

It sounds obvious; we are engaged by doing things we are good at. We only have to look at children to know this is true. Give them something they are interested in and they will do it for hours but if they aren't interested in it they will stick at for only a few minutes, unless they think they might get good at it.

My eldest daughter is a great, but pretty standard example of this. She loves swimming and wants to go swimming as often as possible. However, what she really loves about swimming is backstroke because she is particularly good and fast and wins her races. She is not nearly as good at butterfly and isn't nearly as engaged in these lessons as she is when the lesson is concentrating on getting even better at backstroke.

So it is common sense that we know intuitively; we are motivated and engaged by doing things we are good at. However most big organisations focus on exactly the opposite. They have a competency framework that people are assessed against based on their role and level in the organisation. Where the assessment shows they are weakest the focus of attention rests. It is in this area of weakness that people are trained, supported and coached so that they improve in the area of weakness. The result is standard people in standard roles who all complete the job safely and averagely.

Imagine what could happen if exactly the same assessment took place, but instead of finding the areas of weakness the strengths were identified. Development and training was given in the areas of strength so they became even better in those areas. Roles and responsibilities were moved around so that everyone spent more time doing things they were good at. Each person would come alive and the productivity of the whole organisation would increase dramatically.

There was a great example of the value of understanding our strengths at the 2014 US PGA Golf championship. On the final round Rory McIlroy had lost his overnight one shot lead and was trailing by three shots after the first nine holes. On the par five 10th hole McIlroy drove the green in two shots, the only person in the whole tournament who managed to do so. He then putted for an eagle three catching up the leaders by two shots and creating the momentum that would see him go on and win the championship.

McIlroy's strength is driving straight and long. The rest of his golf game is also very good but it is this strength in driving that makes him unique, different and better than the opposition and it is this strength that is a focus of McIlroy in training. The rest of his game needs practice as weakness leads to failure, but it is our areas of strength that lead to success.

Our culture focuses on weakness due to an unhealthy fear of failure. However it is by focusing on strengths that people will come alive and we will succeed individually and corporately.

The Scientists and Bin Men

A few years ago I was involved in two consulting projects running in parallel. The first was with the street cleaners and bin men of a city in England. The project was to introduce more efficient working processes and improve the effectiveness of the leadership team. The second was with a high tech science organisation. They were the result of the merger of two previous businesses and the work was post-merger to develop a new single culture and efficient and productive working practices. The science undertaken quite literally blew me away and I certainly didn't understand it, but when someone shows you round buildings and equipment with names that sound as if they are straight out of Star Trek, you can't help but be impressed even if you have no idea what they are talking about!

On the surface the two projects looked very different; bin men in one project and some of the world's leading scientists in the other. However the issues with both projects largely came down to good people promoted into management without necessarily being good managers. In both cases we created improvement projects and identified an internal lead for each of the projects. We then did an exercise to identify and showcase the strengths of the teams. The project leads were then asked to choose people to help them on their projects based on what they now understood about each other's strengths.

I was leading on this part of the work for the project with the Bin Men and grown men quite literally cried as their peers recognised their strengths and chose them to help on the projects based on their unique strengths. Both projects were hugely successful and showed that focusing on strengths is incredibly powerful whatever your role, academic ability or walk in life.

Some our strengths have been with us since we were born, others we discover, and in some cases they develop as we grow and mature. Ever since I was young, a strength of mine has been sport. It didn't matter what type of sport but as long as it involved running and a ball of some shape I have always had a natural talent for it and a passion to get even better. A particular strength I now have, which I didn't even know about until I started work as a consultant, is summarising. It sounds quite a small and niche strength, and it probably is, but I've found I have a natural ability. In one to one or group situations I am really good at taking in all of the disparate views and points and pulling it together into a concise summary of the discussion, conversation or agreement. This started off as a natural ability, as I had never been trained in it, and over time I have got better as I have pushed myself to do this in more challenging situations and with larger groups; all of which has helped me to turn this ability into a strength.

We need to understand our strengths so we can develop them further and use them more. There are some good tools available to help you identify your strengths but in the absence of them spend some time thinking through the following questions:

What natural talents / strengths do you have?

How do you currently use these strengths in your work?

What do you do to invest in these strengths and get even better in them?

What else could you do to invest in these strengths?

What could you do to use your strengths more?

Leading others in their strengths

Marcus Buckingham[1] suggests the world's greatest leaders believe that with enough development and investment, a person can achieve anything they set their mind to. Instead of helping people to overcome their weaknesses, great leaders find out what a person likes to do and is good at and empowers them to do work they excel at.

We need to adopt the same approach. We need to help others to understand their strengths; we need to understand their strengths and we need to create opportunities for them to develop into these areas of strength.

Liz Wiseman found that great leaders are multipliers[2]. They actually improve the intelligence and capabilities of those around them by two times. Multipliers look beyond their own ability and instead focus their energy on extracting and extending the ability of others. Wiseman found that they don't get a little more by doing this, they get vastly more. She found that leaders, whom she termed diminishers, stifled others and diluted the organisation's intelligence and capabilities. Effectively staff whose leaders were diminishers were working at 50% their capacity.

We become multipliers by focusing on the strengths of those around us and helping them to focus on their strengths as well. With a combination of concentrating on their strengths and helping them to understand their own vision, we will engage and enthuse our staff. To do this means we have to accept there will be mistakes and failure and that the achievement of our vision isn't the number one objective anymore.

Look for strength not competence

It is important not to confuse strengths with competence when looking for others' strengths so that you can invest in them. A strength comes from a natural ability or inclination and then needs further development to become a recognisable strength. This means that someone's area of strength may not be immediately recognisable because, in actual fact, they aren't that good at it yet in comparison to others.

So looking for strengths to invest in is not as simple as looking for things people are good at. If that were the case there would be no way anyone would develop into areas they had never tried!

References

1. Buckingham, M. (1999) First Break all the Rules, Simon and Schuster

2. Wiseman, L. (2010) Multipliers, How the best leaders make everyone smarter, HarperBusiness

CHAPTER 9

Involvement

To be engaged we need to be involved in things that impact on us

For people to be truly engaged they have to be involved in things that impact on them. We see this time and time again on change programmes that we run. If people have been involved in the process and listened to, then they are far more likely to roll their sleeves up and join in with the implementation, even if they don't agree with the decision!

There was one particular change programme we ran for the Estates and Facilities department of a large NHS Trust, where this was very evident. The Director wanted to change things as he knew there were efficiency savings that could be made, but the department had been very resistant to change and used their experience and expertise in the areas of estates and facilities, to convince the Director, whose background wasn't in this area, that there was no way any change would work. Knowing this background we used the people from the department to design the change programme. Our role was to point them in the right direction and facilitate the process, but they did the work. In the end, the department, that had said no change was possible, found £2million savings from a £10million budget and delivered a better service at the end. They were involved and therefore they bought into it and made it far more successful that anyone envisaged.

To be engaged we also need to understand why we are important and significant. Why is our role vital to the bigger picture? If we understand why we are needed and significant, we are again more likely to be engaged.

Involvement and empowerment have to be undertaken authentically for them to result in increased motivation and engagement. Many staff in large corporates have a very cynical view of involvement. They are 'consulted' about changes, but in fact everyone already knows that the decision has been made. This form of 'consultation' is common and isn't about the organisation, it is normally about the leader. Their view of leadership is that as the leader, they are the one with the ideas and vision and therefore must ultimately make the decision, or have their way.

This type of involvement can be detrimental to the relationship that exists between the leader and everyone else. However the real impact of it is in the long term as it creates followers rather than new leaders. It tells people that their role is to serve the vision of someone else rather than have their own vision. It creates people who give the bare minimum and as a result are robbed of getting the most out of their time at work and who don't give their all.

We need to move from involvement and consultation to empowerment so we reproduce leaders who will have impact rather than followers who serve our visions.

A definition of empowerment that I quite like is that it is about; "sharing degrees of power with lower level employees to better serve the customer."[1]

Empowerment is certainly about sharing power and not just sharing tasks. Very often we think we are empowering by delegating key tasks to people. However, the fact we are delegating tasks means we are not actually being empowering, we are just asking people to complete tasks that we have already thought about and planned. Instead we need to delegate authority. By delegating authority we are telling people; 'I trust you to do a good job here'. We are actually sharing power, a key aspect of this definition. The definition also has a second part; the power is shared for a reason and that reason is to serve an end goal; to better serve the customer.

The definition is saying, and rightly so, that the best way to serve a customer, which is the ultimate aim of the business, is to empower each staff member to make whatever decision is needed to serve the customer at that particular moment. Have you ever called a customer service department to solve a problem for you and there has been a really obvious solution that you have known and that the person on the other end of the phone has known as well? However, despite you both knowing this, the customer service rep hasn't been able to help you because they hadn't been given the authority to; it 'went against company processes'?

A few years ago I was driving to a client's offices and stopped to fill my car up with diesel. It was early in the morning and I mistakenly filled it up with petrol instead. I didn't realise to begin with and carried on driving for about half a mile until my car cut out on the side of the road. I called the break down service. They got to me really quickly and, whilst they were coming, I worked out what I had done. They towed me to the offices of the client I was working with that day, and arranged for their fuel truck to come and drain my fuel tank whilst I was working, brilliant service! The fuel truck guy did what he had to do; I finished my days work and got back in the car to drive home. All was fine until halfway home my car stopped again. I waited three hours this time for the breakdown service. They got to me and found out that the fuel pump guy had put something back in my car the wrong way round. This meant I had been leaking diesel the whole way and I had broken down because I had run out of fuel.

The breakdown guy was great, gave me the number to call to put in a complaint and suggested that I should get a refund for the cost of the fuel I had lost and possibly the cost of the fuel pump work as it hadn't been done right and had led to a great inconvenience. In total this would have all come to about £300.

I duly followed the process he suggested, put in the complaint and was told to wait for an offer of compensation to be sent to me. I waited a week or so and finally a letter came in the post offering me £15 as a sign of goodwill! I wasn't too pleased and I'm ashamed to say I didn't really feel the goodwill at that point in time! I called the company and ended up speaking to a customer service rep who had no authority to do anything other than to stick to the offer in the letter. It was one of the most frustrating phone calls I have ever had and it probably was for them as well. I clearly explained the inconvenience caused, the cost of the fuel I had lost and the fact it was because their staff hadn't done their job properly that all of this had happened. This last part wasn't quite true as if I had put the correct fuel in in the first place the whole situation would have been avoided.

The poor customer service rep completely agreed with everything I said, but wasn't empowered to do anything beyond what the letter said. A few days later I spoke to their manager who had more authority and we reached a compromise somewhere between the two values. The manager had the authority to make that decision, which made me happy and meant that their job was actually far more pleasant than the original poor rep. I asked the manager why the original person wasn't able to do what they had done and I got the standard company reply, they don't have authorisation to do that sort of thing.

If we delegate authority and empower people by giving away power, we actually achieve the end goals far more effectively. The end goals, based on the definition above, are providing the best service for customers.

Creating an empowering environment

Really empowering people as the norm is rare in my experience. People talk about it and do it in degrees, but really giving power and control away and taking the risk that goes with that is rare. Sometimes the leader at the top may do it, but people further down the organisational structure then become barriers to developing a truly engaging culture as they don't follow in the same path set by the leader. The following are important features of an engaging culture:

Transparent sharing of information – sharing information is important because it not only helps to build trust; it gives employees important information that will allow them to make the best possible decisions in critical situations. Communication, or sharing of information, is often the first hurdle to empowerment as 'information is power'. It is easy to slip into a subconscious mind set of controlling people through the power we have as we have more information than they do. Often we use information to keep people down without realising it, because we think it is the right thing to do. However, whatever the reason, it doesn't raise people up and empower them. In many organisations I've worked with senior managers who keep much of the unpleasant information about a change programme to themselves, because they think their staff can't handle it. What they don't realise is that the biggest complaint of their staff is not that there will be some unpleasant changes, but that they are being treated like children as it is presumed that they can't cope with bad news.

A few years ago we had a piece of work for a large local authority of one of the major cities in the UK. They had gone through a far reaching change programme and it was going very badly. At the root of the problem was gossip. Wherever you went in the organisation you heard gossip that; 'this is going to happen' or 'that is going to happen', 'they will change this next' or 'they will change that next'. No one knew exactly what was going to happen and in the absence of information, stories were made up that created fear, led to demotivation and resulted in productivity levels dropping massively. I'm sure that, if you've worked for a large organisation, you can relate to this story. In times of change the lack of information acts as a catalyst for gossip, fear and demotivation. After university I took a year out and worked for a charity. My boss was a Glaswegian called Iain Bruce who had sayings about everything. One of them was; "when communication breaks down the imagination runs wild".

This is so true and is exactly what happened in this case.

The local authority recruited a new interim Chief Executive who I will call Mike Jones for the purpose of this. He quickly realised that stopping the gossip was the single most important thing he had to do. He started to meet with all staff fortnightly, which was pretty much a full time job as there were around 12,000 staff. When he met with them he said to them; *"I'm going to be completely open and honest about everything that is going to happen and everything that is happening. If you ask me a question I will tell you the answer if I know it, even if you might not like the answer. However, in return I want you to do something for me. The next time you hear someone say something about the changes that are happening, say to them, 'did Mike Jones tell you that?' If they can't say yes or you don't believe them, then don't pass that information on."*

Quite soon you heard people regularly saying, "Did Mike Jones tell you that?" and it became a bit of a joke around the place. However it worked! Pretty soon Mike moved the meetings to monthly and then quarterly. Motivation increased and the whole programme got back on track. Why? Because information was used to empower people rather than control them.

Positive risk taking – we need to create a culture that says that it's OK to make mistakes, because it is only by making mistakes that we learn and we do new things. Many of the organisations that I work with are crippled by fear. People won't try anything above and beyond the absolute standard because of fear that they will be blamed and possibly lose their job if it goes wrong. This has such a negative effect on people as the culture that develops stops them from being the people they could be.

Positive risk taking is about managing risk rather than completely avoiding it. The bigger mistake is often the over reaction from the original mistake.

Celebrate successes and failures – as part of creating a culture of empowerment we need to celebrate our successes and celebrate what we have learned from trying things that didn't work out. The act of trying something new should be encouraged and praised.

Empowerment self-assessment

Have a look at the table below. Reflect on the statements and choose a rating that reflects how frequently it applies to you.

	A lot of the time	Some of the time	Very little / none of the time
I allow others the freedom to develop their own visions and pursue them			
I actively try to raise people who are gifted and talented above and beyond me			
I provide encouragement and make myself available for support			
I help others to learn from their mistakes in a non-critical setting			
I seek feedback from others to find out how I can improve			
I stand back and allow others to take credit for their efforts			
I coach others to help them work out the answers for themselves			
I encourage others to be creative and take appropriate risks			
I actively seek opportunities to develop others			

References

1. Knicki, A. & Kreitner, R. (2008), Organisational Behaviour, Mcgraw Hill

CHAPTER10

So what next?

This book is about how to create an engaging leadership culture that quite literally brings people and organisations to life.

When people are engaged they have energy, ideas, creativity and the will to take the initiative and increase their effort. The positive impact this has on a business is as obvious as it is large. However, the positive impact on the individual is also marked. They enjoy their work! Considering the percentage of time we spend at work this isn't something to be down played. People truly can enjoy their work, experience reduced stress and find meaning and purpose in what they are doing and the relationships they have at work.

So the benefits of engagement are on both sides; the employer and the employee. The employer get more effort for the wage they pay out whilst the employee finds increased satisfaction and meaning.

So why don't we do it better? This is a good question that to answer it fully requires a journey back into history and the development of leadership theories in the modern age. A more useful question is: what can we do to change things?

Changing engagement levels in a meaningful way requires a change of culture, particularly the leadership cultures that exist in our orgaisations. That is what this book is about; identifying the leadership cultures that impact on engagement and looking at ways to develop and implement these positive cultures within our organisations.

This change starts with us and will quickly be followed by others that see the change in us and also decide to model a new way of leading.

It has to happen to maintain competitiveness and respond to the many challenges we face in our markets today. When it does happen, the impact is great and can be measured in a way that demonstrates return on investment and impact on the bottom line.

The next step is to increase the engaging nature of your own leadership. Use this book to remind and inspire you. Gather others around you who also know the need for change. Use this book to create a common language and support each other to make the changes personally and in the teams that you lead. Over time things will change, but it requires sustained effort.

Enjoy the journey, but more importantly take satisfaction from seeing your organisations grow as you grow your people through engagement.

For more information on the author and further tools and support provided to develop cultures of engagement visit:

www.engage-deep.co.uk

Lightning Source UK Ltd.
Milton Keynes UK
UKOW06f1537090415

249375UK00007B/162/P